Building Bridges
From **Early** to **Intermediate**
Literacy
Grades 2–4

We dedicate this book to our families and friends whose support and belief in us were an important part of this work.

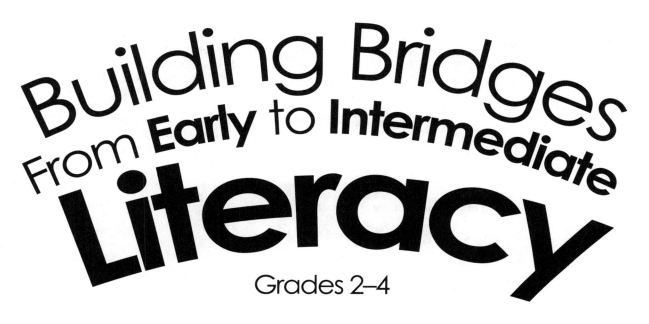

Building Bridges
From Early to Intermediate
Literacy
Grades 2–4

Sarah F. Mahurt • Ruth E. Metcalfe • Margaret A. Gwyther
Foreword by Margaret Mooney

CORWIN PRESS
A SAGE Publications Company
Thousand Oaks, CA 91320

For information:

Corwin Press
A Sage Publications Company
2455 Teller Road
Thousand Oaks, California 91320
www.corwinpress.com

Sage Publications Ltd.
1 Oliver's Yard
55 City Road
London, EC1Y 1SP
United Kingdom

SAGE Publications India Pvt. Ltd.
B 1/I 1 Mohan Cooperative
    Industrial Area
Mathura Road, New Delhi 110 044
India

SAGE Publications Asia-Pacific Pte. Ltd.
33 Pekin Street #02-01
Far East Square
Singapore 048763

Printed in the United States of America

Library of Congress Cataloging-in-Publication Data

Mahurt, Sarah F.
Building bridges from early to intermediate literacy, grades 2–4/
Sarah F. Mahurt, Ruth E. Metcalfe, and Margaret A. Gwyther.
    p. cm.
Includes bibliographical references and index.
ISBN 978-1-4129-4962-0 (cloth)
ISBN 978-1-4129-4963-7 (pbk.)
    1. Language arts (Primary) 2. English language—Composition and exercises—Study and teaching (Primary) 3. Active learning. I. Metcalfe, Ruth E. II. Gwyther, Margaret A. III. Title.
LB1528.M284 2007
372.6—dc22   2007002113

This book is printed on acid-free paper.

07 08 09 10 11 10 9 8 7 6 5 4 3 2 1

Acquisitions Editor:	Cathy Hernandez
Editorial Assistants:	Jordan Barbakow
	Megan Bedell
Production Editor:	Beth A. Bernstein
Copy Editor:	Carla Freeman
Typesetter:	C&M Digitals (P) Ltd.
Proofreader:	Dennis W. Webb
Indexer:	Karen McKenzie
Cover Designer:	Lisa Miller

Contents

List of Figures

Foreword

REFLECTIONS OF A READER

A good book is a good book! A good book confirms as well as extends one's understandings about a topic, a theme, and an issue. A good book engenders and supports comprehension at literal, inferential, and analytical levels. A good book tells (literal); it causes thought beyond the stated (inferential); and it leads to an awareness of new understandings, to a decision, or to action (analytical). The clarity of text and content in *Building Bridges From Early to Intermediate Literacy, Grades 2–4*, eased and enhanced my understandings at all three levels. And in doing so, it caused me to reflect on bridges built and safely crossed in recent years.

Recent surges in research, accountability, and legislation have established both the need and a blueprint for bridges between the old and new, the extremities of methods, and the divisive organizations within schools. The subsequent revitalized professional development opportunities highlight both the privileges and responsibilities of teaching literacy. And it is those opportunities and responsibilities that this book celebrates.

As a good book is a good book, so is a good teacher a good teacher! *Building Bridges From Early to Intermediate Literacy, Grades 2–4*, claims to focus on the "in-between" years, and at a literal level, it does a fine job of guiding the building of an intentional and balanced research-based literacy program for students in the "in-between" phase, straddling the acquisition and application of skills confidently and competently.

At an inferential level, the reading becomes more personal, provoking consideration of implications. As I became absorbed in the reading, my thinking moved from specific grades to an appreciation of a teacher's role in a student's continuous journey as a literate learner. The focus on the "in-between" years provided the range and depth of consideration, but the structure and areas of consideration provide a framework for every level. It is not what a teacher does at any level that supports literacy development, but how a teacher builds bridges from what is in place to what is to come that makes a good teacher into an even better one.

As I completed my first reading of the manuscript, I realized that my conversation with and through the text had been as if I were in the classrooms described in the book and the authors were in the classrooms in which I work. Our evaluative conversation had clearly identified action I needed to take, so my second reading was more selective and analytical. The three levels of comprehension I had experienced as I read the book were exactly those through which a good teacher prompts and guides his or her students from dependence to independence.

So, acknowledging the role of a foreword in preparing the readers for what is to come, or, more important, for the conversation they might have with the authors, I advise that although this book may appear to be an easy read, it may not be a totally comfortable one. There is no learning without moments of discomfort, and the forthright manner in which good practices are expounded in this book will cause moments of evaluative reflection and challenges for resolve and action. There will surely be pointers for new bridges to be built, but the plans are clear and the pathways illuminated: a model in itself for intentional and focused instruction—the topic, theme, and issue of this book.

—Margaret Mooney

Preface

A second-grade classroom teacher said, "Resources for primary literacy learners are great, but most of my kids have those early reading and writing strategies under control, and the activities recommended for older kids are way too complex. What am I supposed to do to get my readers and writers from where they are now to where they need to be in the intermediate grades?"

The idea for this book grew from many teachers' questions and concerns like the one above, about preparing primary children for the literacy expectations of the intermediate grades. Teachers feel they currently have many resources focused on beginning reading and writing that provide an instructional paradigm most effective in kindergarten and first grade. At the same time, there are growing numbers of resources focused on instruction that seems more appropriate for the intermediate grades. Teachers in second and third grade believe they have been overlooked and left to adapt either a primary- or intermediate-literacy model that fails to meet the specific needs of all the children in their classrooms. In this book, we attempt to provide clarity and guidance for teachers who work with children in the later primary grades so they may more effectively support children in becoming more competent intermediate readers and writers.

In addition, the National Reading Panel (2001) has set an instructional agenda for literacy development that teachers are implementing in their classrooms, and No Child Left Behind requirements have raised the bar for the literacy development of all elementary children across the country. Teachers are working hard, using all the resources available to them to ensure that their students meet these changing literacy requirements. Unfortunately, many teachers in Grades 2 and 3 are discovering that resources addressing the needs of their students are not easily found. They feel stuck in the middle. Our intention for this book is to assist teachers to more easily build bridges in literacy learning for children as they transition from the primary to the intermediate grades.

We approach this challenge as educators who have faced the issue of knowing the differing needs of our learners as they grow, while continually reflecting on how best to meet those needs. One author, Ruth, when transferred from teaching first grade to second grade, has experienced the frustration of trying to find resources that specifically address the needs of literacy learners in Grades 2 and 3. Peg and Sarah have years of experience in several states working with teachers at various grade levels who also expressed the feeling of being left to adapt a primary-literacy model while at the same time modifying an intermediate instructional framework, neither of which fits the learning needs of their students.

Because of these concerns, we decided to more closely explore teaching in Grades 2 and 3 as a way to help teachers work with students in those grades. We emphasize the instruction and learning necessary to transition from the primary to the intermediate grades. We hope to provide guidance and support for teachers as they build a bridge for primary children to become competent readers and writers in the intermediate grades.

In Chapter 1, we begin with a brief explanation of our underlying beliefs about learning and instruction, including meeting the needs of diverse learners. We provide an overview of some of the changes children make in literacy learning as they progress from the primary grades to intermediate grades, and we discuss the instructional tools that teachers find useful during this time of transition.

In Chapter 2, we focus on assessment as the basis for understanding literacy growth and planning for effective instruction. Knowing what changes to make in instruction and how to implement those changes comes through understanding individual students. Ongoing formal and informal assessment is vital to informing instructional decisions over the course of the year.

Chapters 3, 4, and 5 highlight instructional approaches for meeting the literacy development needs of students in the transition process from primary to intermediate grades in each of three specific areas. While we believe that literacy processes are linked to each other and more powerfully taught when taught together, we divide the book into the areas of word study, reading, and writing to present more detail about instruction in each of those areas of literacy development and learning.

In Chapter 3, we focus on word study and include instruction in phonics and phonemic awareness, structural analysis, and vocabulary development, as well as continuing development of a strong core of high-frequency words. This chapter emphasizes shifts in word study as children move from using mostly letter/sound relationships to using more complex vowel and consonant patterns. It includes active use of word walls and word study charts.

Chapter 4 addresses the shifts in reading instruction that occur as children become more competent readers. We first discuss the changing needs and capabilities of readers and then suggest how the reading workshop format would change to meet the needs of readers moving toward becoming more independent as processors of text. Attention is given to management and instructional issues, knowing when and how to make shifts, and using assessments to guide teacher decision making.

In Chapter 5, we describe the changes young writers make as writing becomes a more fluent and deliberate act. There is a focus on shifts in instruction related to the composition and transcription needs of transitional writers. This chapter includes goal setting, teaching for independence, and using assessments to determine the teacher's instructional focus. In addition, we address the need for shifts in writing workshop minilessons and conferences as students become more competent, confident writers.

Whereas these three chapters look in depth at specific parts of literacy learning and instruction, Chapter 6 pulls these processes back together, demonstrating ways to connect learning across the language arts as well as link literacy to content-area instruction. This deliberate linking allows for more powerful, effective teaching and learning, and it facilitates the type of literacy work expected in intermediate grades as the foundation for life-long learning. In addition, this linking emphasizes the application of reading and writing in all areas of the curriculum and enables teachers to streamline instruction, making efficient use of classroom time.

Our intention is to fill a gap in understanding and practice in literacy learning and to support and possibly simplify the lives of our teacher colleagues and friends. You are the ones who are making a difference in the lives of our children and therefore our futures. We honor and respect all that you do and hope this book will assist you in ways no other book has been able to accomplish.

Acknowledgments

We would like to acknowledge our editor Cathy Hernandez and her assistant Megan Bedell for their advice and support. We would also like to acknowledge Carla Freeman for her fine editing. Our deep and heartfelt appreciation goes to all the teachers and literacy coordinators who shared with us their experiences, their knowledge, and their wishes for a resource devoted to children in Grades 2 and 3. We want to thank all the children who allowed us to work with and observe them. Without all of you, we would not have been able to write this book.

PUBLISHER'S ACKNOWLEDGMENTS

Corwin Press gratefully acknowledges the contributions of the following reviewers:

Tammy Ashbeck
Principal
Highland Hills Elementary
   School
Hermiston, OR

Sarah Baird
Academic Interventionist
Kyrene School District
   No. 28
Chandler, AZ

Amy Blocher
Reading Coach
Bartow Middle School
   and Compass Middle
   Charter School
Bartow, FL

Amy Broemmel
Assistant Professor of Theory
   and Practice in Teacher
   Education
University of Tennessee
Knoxville, TN

Christine Clement
Third Grade Teacher
Woodlake Elementary School
Mandeville, LA

Jolene Dockstader
Literacy Coach and English
   Language Arts Teacher
Jerome Middle School
Jerome, ID

Debbie Halcomb
Third and Fourth Grade
  Teacher
R. W. Combs Elementary
  School
Happy, KY

Michael Ice
Second Grade Teacher
Sanders Elementary
Louisville, KY

Laura Linde
Literacy Coach
Hoover Elementary
North Mankato, MN

Alexis Ludewig
Resource Teacher
Saint Germain Elementary
  School
Saint Germain, WI

Vickie McCullah
Reading First Director
Howe Elementary
  School
Howe, OK

Marci Rossi
Third Grade Teacher
Booksin Elementary School
San Jose, CA

About the Authors

Sarah F. Mahurt is the director of the Purdue Literacy Collaborative and associate professor of Literacy and Language at Purdue. Through her leadership, the Purdue Literacy Collaborative has trained more than 80 literacy coordinators to be literacy leaders and coaches in their schools. This project has reached more than 800 teachers, who are improving their teaching of literacy and student achievement in literacy. She recently received the Department of Curriculum and Instruction's Engagement Award for this school reform effort.

Sarah's publications include articles on the integration of reading and writing, teacher development, and Caribbean children's literature. She has also made numerous presentations on literacy teaching and learning in elementary schools and school reform in literacy education. She has consulted with schools and districts, focusing on schools improving student achievement in reading and writing. She recently chaired a committee to develop a statewide network of educators in Indiana who are focused on improving writing instruction.

In more than 25 years as an educator, Sarah has worked as a classroom teacher, reading specialist, and university professor. She was awarded the Celebrate Literacy Award from the St. Croix Chapter of the International Reading Association and the Alpha Kappa Alpha Outstanding Educator Award for her literacy work in St. Croix, Virgin Islands. She also received the Teaching Excellence Award at the University of the Virgin Islands.

Ruth E. Metcalfe has been a literacy coordinator and teacher for Goshen Community Schools in Goshen, Indiana. She has a master's degree in elementary education, and she completed a yearlong course to become a literacy coordinator. During her 16 years as an educator, she has taught first, second, and fourth grades and provided professional development and coaching at the building level. She is currently released from teaching to work full-time with all first- and second-year primary teachers and to provide support to other primary-literacy coordinators throughout the district.

In addition to her work as a teacher and staff developer, Ruth has been a literacy consultant for elementary schools. She has presented at national conferences, with a focus on reading and writing in second grade as a transition to the intermediate grades. She has also presented at state conferences on comprehension and language development.

Ruth has completed action research in her own classroom to determine the impact of her learning on her practice. She also researched the impact of Literacy Collaborative on first graders in her school, looking at English language learners and children who were new to the school.

Ruth infuses her classroom with joyful and powerful teaching. She also enjoys working with teachers on how theory looks when put into practice in the classroom—the place where theory and practice meet. She is passionate about literacy, children, teaching, and learning.

Margaret Ann Gwyther is a national literacy consultant and coach. She facilitates adult learning through ongoing professional development and coaching. She has been a keynote presenter at local, state, regional, national, and international conferences, focusing on literacy, Reading Recovery, and distance delivery technology, and she consults with universities, schools, and school districts throughout the country to provide ongoing assistance in improving literacy instruction and children's learning. She spent eight years training coaches through Literacy Collaborative at the Ohio State University and Purdue University.

Margaret's wide range of experiences in teaching, coaching, and education administration are the basis for her intense interest in children's literacy and learning, as well as the professional development of teachers. She has been an elementary teacher, a middle school and high school athletic coach, a high school activity director and vice principal, a Reading Recovery teacher leader, and a professional development director.

Margaret has traveled extensively, leading students on athletic tours and teachers on education tours in various foreign countries. She established the Alaska Distance Delivery pilot project in collaboration with the Ohio State University, for training Reading Recovery teachers in villages and communities across the state and above the Arctic Circle. These experiences provide a strong base for understanding how schools work, the development of teachers, and children's learning.

1

Introduction

A first-grade classroom hums with activity as students and teacher settle into the work of reading. Children in the far corner of the room sort pictures by the ending sounds of words represented in the pictures, while their classmates nearby use magnetic letters to build words found on the word wall. At the overhead projector, another small group is rereading a poem they learned earlier in the week, circling words they know. One child stands at the easel, using a pointer to track print in a big book as two others follow along, chanting the words to this familiar story. Near the back of the room, two girls excitedly share ideas for the letters they are writing to the school librarian, telling her the dates of their birthdays. They decide together how to spell the librarian's name and refer to the word wall for other words they need. In the library corner, one child sits quietly, looking through a pile of books he has pulled from the shelves. He is looking for words he knows in the books. The rest of the children at this station are poring over the pictures in the book read aloud to the class by their teacher at the start of the workshop time. They are retelling the story and are able to read the repeated phrases in the book when they come to those pages. Along one wall near the middle of the room, the teacher sits at a low table with four students who have similar needs for reading development. She introduces a new book to them and supports them as they each negotiate the text. As they finish, the group discusses the book and engages in a brief word study activity. The classroom is alive with energy and purposeful noise, and children ask each other for help, asking the teacher only when she is not working with a group at the guided-reading table. The sounds of children's voices reading, negotiating, and explaining are evidence of high engagement in activities designed to support learning of early reading behaviors and strategies.

Down the hall, a class of third graders has also begun their reading workshop. The teacher taught a minilesson on how characters often change in response to events in a story. During the minilesson, she and the children discussed how they noticed this in the chapter book the teacher had been reading aloud over the past week. They decided to look for characters that change in the different books they will be reading independently. Then, over the next few days, when they meet to discuss their reading, they will share what they individually recorded in their reading-response logs. As the children settle into the reading workshop time, the classroom is hushed, and any necessary conversation is done in whispers. Several children find spots on the floor, taking with them one or two longer texts that they quickly begin reading. Others opt to read at their desks, a few taking out their reading logs in order to write down their thoughts as they read. Four children gather quietly near the door of the classroom, each carrying a copy of the same text, sticky notes waving like flags from the pages. They quickly decide who will speak first as they begin their literature circle discussion. After briefly conferring with one or two students, the teacher taps the shoulders of three students, who join her at a table in the back of the room. She has noticed that all three are struggling to determine the main idea of what they are reading and has decided to form a temporary guided-reading group to provide instruction and extra support. After meeting with one or two other guided-reading groups and conferring with a few more students individually, the teacher calls the class back together to share what they have learned in their independent reading about ways characters change. During the workshop time, it is rare for a child to need peer or teacher assistance. As the children and teacher work, the classroom is quiet and focused, with most children processing and responding to text independently or in small groups.

There are many differences in student work, expectations, and activities in these snapshots of two classes engaged in reading workshop. As children move into the intermediate grades, they need different instructional contexts. Many teachers feel stuck in the middle between the expectations and differences they see between first- and third-grade learners, and they are looking for resources to guide their work as they help learners transition from the primary to intermediate grades.

Calkins (1994) and her colleagues noticed similar issues surrounding second- and third-grade learners. As the researchers talked with second- and third-grade teachers, they came to label this age group as "in between" (p. 109). They also compared this "in between" age as being similar to early adolescence, with "emotional, physical, psychological, and intellectual" (p. 109) changes taking place. These changes also include social changes such that the children begin to worry what others think about them and their work in school. Students at this age want what they do to be right.

In addition to focusing on the instructional needs and contexts of learners transitioning from the primary grades to the intermediate grades, we have infused themes of teaching for strategic action, independence, and meeting the needs of diverse learners throughout the book. Many teachers tell us their students know what to do as readers and writers when working with support but seem unable to demonstrate that same knowledge and ability when working independently on school tasks or on high-stakes tests. We believe children need to learn to be independent problem solvers, and we, as their teachers, must help them achieve that goal through our use of an instructional design for gradual release of responsibility. Not only must the nature of support we provide change over time as children engage in reading and writing more complex texts, but we also need to change the content of that support. We want to be sure the language we use as we work with readers and writers is language supportive of independence and not dependence. This is an area in which we continue to struggle. We need to support students in making a more gradual transition from explicit instruction to independent application by providing numerous and varied opportunities for shared and guided practice. This shared and guided practice may occur in whole-class or small-group instruction, following direct teaching or in working individually with students. During this time, the teacher participates with the children, prompting them to take action, guiding their responses, and providing feedback on their attempts.

TEACHING FOR INDEPENDENCE

One way to move children to independence is through a model of gradual release of responsibility (Duke & Pearson, 2002). *Gradual release of responsibility* means that the application of new knowledge progresses from explicit instruction with high teacher support to independent application with no teacher support. Instruction moves from activities that require modeling of a strategic activity, to engaging learners through shared and guided practice, to finally involving learners in opportunities for independent application. Figure 1.1 outlines the concept of gradual release of responsibility and shows how the levels of teacher support change with different instructional experiences and contexts. For example, the teacher provides explicit instruction and models, providing high support in contexts such as reading aloud and mini-lessons. Teachers provide less support, and children take on more responsibility as readers and writers during instructional elements such as guided reading and interactive writing. During independent practice, children use what they have learned, and the teacher observes. A key part of this shift toward independence is the teacher's expectation that children will take on responsibility for using what they know. While children are working independently, the teacher observes and assesses the processes and products that demonstrate how children are reading and writing without teacher support. These observations and assessments form the foundation for future instructional decisions.

TEACHING FOR STRATEGIC ACTION

As we teach for independence, we also need to teach children to take strategic action as readers and writers. Strategic action involves using literacy

Figure 1.1   Gradual Release of Responsibility

Learning new knowledge and applying only through teacher support, demonstration, and modeling	Applying knowledge with teacher prompting and limited support	Applying knowledge with no teacher prompting or support
High Teacher Support		Low Teacher Support
• Teacher-directed lessons in reading, writing, word study • Modeling and demonstration • Small, needs-based groups	• Teaching and support in workshops and guided reading and writing • Focused application in interactive writing and shared reading • Shared experiences and activities	• Small-group practice during independent work stations • Individual practice in reading and writing • Application in independent reading and writing
Instructional Contexts: Read aloud Reading minilessons Writing minilessons Word study minilessons	*Instructional Contexts:* Shared reading Shared writing Interactive writing Guided reading Writing workshop Reading workshop	*Instructional Contexts:* Independent reading Independent writing Independent practice of word study skills Projects/presentations/products

SOURCE: Adapted from Fountas and Pinnell (1996) and Diller (2003).

knowledge and an understanding of how language works in reading and writing. Clay (2001) discusses strategic action as a process where the reader (or writer) uses his or her literacy knowledge to gather information from the text, works on it, makes a decision, evaluates that decision, and makes corrections as necessary. This happens in the brain at split-second speed. In reading, a reader is taking strategic action when she monitors what she reads on a continual basis to check on herself, confirm or detect an error, and self-correct using problem-solving abilities. As part of this strategic action, she knows when and how to use her knowledge of letter sounds, words, and text. In writing, a writer takes strategic action when he uses his understandings of letters and letter sounds, grammar, and word meaning, along with knowledge of text structures, to produce a text. These strategies are patterns for thinking and applying knowledge to accomplish a task (Mooney, 2004). To be strategic as a reader or writer, a person must use knowledge about literacy, such as letter names and sounds or word meaning, along with knowledge of how books work in order to problem solve literacy events. Routman (1991) explains the difference between teaching skills (knowledge about reading and writing) and teaching children to take strategic action as knowing "how and when to apply the skill" (p. 135). It is this idea of teaching children to use their skills "purposefully and independently" (p. 135) that moves children to develop as independent problem solvers in literacy. This is our goal as literacy teachers.

STRUGGLING READERS AND ENGLISH LANGUAGE LEARNERS

We understand that the changes in literacy challenges in primary grades to literacy challenges in intermediate grades can be a major leap for all children, but especially for students who have been struggling in their learning or whose first language is not English. One thing is clear: there is no magic pill we can provide to those who struggle while learning to read and write. We would like for there to be one, but no single program will meet the needs of all students or even all the needs of one student. It is the combination of effective teaching in all aspects of literacy instruction that will make a difference.

Struggling readers and writers and English language learners (ELLs) need to be part of whole-class instruction and are supported through activities such as shared reading of grade-level text (McCormack, Paratore, & Dahlene, 2003). These experiences serve as models and can lead student development through the language and support the teacher and class provide. Through explicit instruction with examples and specific language that tell students how to use new learning as readers and writers, we can make whole-group lessons more accessible for all learners. In addition to involving all students in whole-class activities, both struggling readers and ELLs benefit from whole-class and small-group activities such as shared reading and writing, word study, guided reading, independent reading and writing, and explicit comprehension strategy instruction (Ash, 2002). And when word study, reading, and writing instruction are linked, students can use the connections between these language processes to become more successful literacy learners (Mahurt, 2005).

In addition to good classroom instruction for all learners, we should provide individual instruction to meet the specific needs of students. Through assessment, we learn about the knowledge base in reading and writing for each student, the strategic actions they are taking, and where their gaps exist. All children must have instruction that builds on their strengths and is based on their specific and rapidly changing needs. To accelerate learning for students we are worried about, we must pinpoint what they need and teach to that need in order for them to make progress. Without accelerated learning, some children will continue to fall behind and perform below their peers.

To meet individual needs, we should confer more frequently with ELLs and students who are struggling than we do with other students. We can meet with them for reading and writing conferences during independent reading or writing as well as during small-group guided reading and writing. Some students need more instructional time and more time actively engaged in reading, writing, and speaking (Allington, 2000). Providing more frequent individual and small-group instruction allows us to provide specific support that is carefully aimed at specific needs and gives children opportunities to use their new language more comfortably. By carefully observing and monitoring learners, we can adjust our instruction on a daily basis or even moment to moment.

It should be noted that children will make progress at different rates. We must be willing to flexibly group students and continually rethink which children need to be part of which group and why it would be an effective placement at any point in time. With careful use of assessment to plan instruction, students who struggle may progress more quickly and no longer struggle with grade-appropriate material.

In writing this book, our thinking was guided by the underlying beliefs of teaching for strategic action, the gradual release of responsibility toward independence, and the importance of effective instruction for all learners. As we began to think about ways readers and writers change over time and the instructional contexts that might best fit their needs, we consistently kept in mind our overall purpose of developing readers and writers who successfully solve problems when they are working independently.

HOW CHILDREN GROW AS READERS AND WRITERS

To think about instructional changes as children learn and grow, we need to think about how children change as readers and writers as they progress from the end of first grade into the intermediate grades. They change not only in what they know; they change in what they can do. Early readers understand the basic concepts of print and how to use those concepts as readers. They know letters, names, and sounds as well as a pool of high-frequency words. They know word patterns and how to solve simple words they encounter as they read. They understand what they are reading in their simple texts and understand what is read to them from more complex texts. Readers grow from using beginning word-solving strategies in simple texts to more complex problem solving in longer, more difficult texts. As they move from the primary to intermediate grades, they concentrate on reading for longer periods of time and develop stamina to work though more print-dense books. They most often read silently. And because the reading they can do on their own becomes more complex, students apply comprehending strategies for higher levels of understanding, such as inference, synthesis, and analysis, in books they read to themselves. They develop a natural-sounding fluency that goes back and forth between conscious and unconscious use of punctuation, phrasing, and expression, and they vary their rates of reading depending on the purpose for reading and the type of text.

As writers, children go through a similar growth process. Early writers use the basic concepts of print, knowing where to start their writing, what direction to go, and what letters to use in the development of a message. Soon, they begin to have greater control over the application of these basic conventions of print. Their use of punctuation improves and includes quotation marks and commas as well as end marks. As writers grow, they are able to more fluently spell a larger pool of simple, high-frequency words, as well as words with more complex spelling patterns. They are also able to use word-solving strategies to more quickly write unknown words. As the act of writing becomes more automatic, children are able to write for longer periods of time and develop stamina for writing longer texts. As elementary writers develop, they compose longer, more focused pieces, and their stories have more appropriate content and better structure. These writers add details, move text, and further develop specific parts of their stories as part of a revision process. As writers develop, they are more deliberate in their use of voice and use more powerful and precise language. They have more expertise in writing in different genres and focus on composition. Figure 1.2 charts some of the changes children make in literacy learning as they move through elementary school.

Understanding how readers and writers change during this period we refer to as "transition" both informs and guides adjustments in teaching practices. As children move from the primary grades to the intermediate grades, instructional contexts also change. In the chapters that highlight word study, reading, and writing, the changes children make as they grow as readers and writers will be emphasized and tied directly to changes in instruction.

As learners, children transitioning from primary to intermediate grades fall within a wide range of abilities. Some may still be considered beginning readers, while others are capable of handling more complex material. However, all these children are still young and need opportunities to play with and explore language. In the rush to meet standards and improve standardized test scores, we should keep in mind the fundamental need for young children to learn through independent investigations and not just direct instruction provided by the teacher. Teachers must be deliberate in planning activities that not only develop stamina by extending reading and writing times but also allow for exploration, communication, and movement during literacy workshops.

Figure 1.2 Changes Over Time in Literacy Development

	Early Elementary	*Transition*	*Intermediate*
Reading	• Develops basic print concepts • Begins to control early reading strategies and behaviors • Begins to monitor own reading • Self-corrects occasionally • Relies on picture support • Uses limited experience with various genres • Builds a small core of high-frequency words • Reads aloud most of the time • Comprehends basic story line for independently read text • Responds to texts verbally • Demonstrates more complex understanding of texts read aloud • Illustrates as a way to respond to text reading	• Develops and uses a large core of high-frequency words • Strengthens control over early reading behaviors and strategies • Maintains reading for longer periods of time • Develops more complex understanding of texts read independently • Responds to texts both verbally and in writing • Reads silently most of the time • Monitors own reading consistently • Problem solves using a variety of sources of information • Can read a wide variety of genres • Reads more fluently in meaningful phrases with some attention to punctuation • Writes simple responses to texts independently	• Recognizes and accurately uses a large core of known words • Navigates texts subconsciously • Maintains deep understanding of text • Reads for extended periods of time and reads texts over several days • Responds to text both verbally and in writing • Monitors reading; able to flexibly problem solve without losing momentum or meaning • Is familiar with a wide variety of genres • Reads expressively in meaningful phrases with natural-sounding fluency
Writing	• Uses basic narrative structure of familiar topics • Writes a few sentences • Uses simple sentence structure • Thinks consciously about forming words • Uses some conventional spellings of high-frequency words • Uses invented spelling of some complex words • Does little revision or editing • Does little conscious planning • Matches illustrations to text • Uses illustrations to inspire text • Labors to record a message	• Uses basic narrative structure with different topics • Begins to carry pieces over several days • Has variable use of end punctuation; experiments with other punctuation • Has control over a core of high-frequency words • Uses invented spelling of many complex words • Does some editing • Revises, but often limited to adding more text • Uses some planning • Supplements text with illustrations	• Makes deliberate decisions about form and genre • Writes longer pieces of several pages • Uses more complex sentence structures • Uses most end punctuation correctly; uses others variably (e.g., quotation marks, commas, ellipses) • Writes fluently, yet slows for difficult words • Spells most words correctly • Revises and edits • Gives feedback for revision to other writers • Plans writing • Is forming a sense of audience

	Early Elementary	Transition	Intermediate
Word Study	• Has basic knowledge of letter/sound relationships • Knows consonants, blends, short and long vowel patterns in single-syllable words • Uses sound analysis when spelling unknown words • Has a basic writing vocabulary of some high-frequency words • Uses basic vocabulary to express thoughts	• Has knowledge of consonant clusters, more complex visual vowel patterns to represent sounds • Uses inflectional endings, simple suffixes, and compound words • Knows many high-frequency words • Uses sound analysis for spelling unknown words and begins to use visual analysis • Uses more precise vocabulary	• Has basic phonics under control • Understands structural analysis of words, including affixes, root and base words, and multisyllable words • Has high-frequency words under control in both reading and writing tasks • Uses visual analysis and understanding of word structure in spelling • Refines and extends vocabulary

LITERACY INSTRUCTION DURING TRANSITION

Children need to grow as literacy learners, developing the skills and strategies necessary for becoming successful readers and writers. As they leave primary grades, they must also be able to meet the challenges of the intermediate grades. Teachers need to provide experiences to develop independence and sustained control over a variety of reading and writing tasks. The focus of instruction progressively changes as assessments and observations show that children need different practices to continue their growth as readers and writers.

Figure 1.3 illustrates a variety of instructional tools to help children transition from early literacy learning to a more intermediate focus. Teachers provide more direct support in the primary grades through interactive writing, shared reading, and small-group guided reading. As a transition to more independent literature discussion, teachers model and lead discussions during and after "read alouds" and later guide children's literature response in small groups before moving to independent literature discussion groups. More time is given to independent reading and response to reading as children develop the ability to work independently for longer periods of time, reading longer texts and writing longer pieces. In writing, as children gain control over the basic knowledge of how to write words, the focus moves from daily interactive and shared writing with emphasis on both transcription and composition elements to a more singular focus on composition and craft. Writing workshop becomes longer as children are able to write for longer periods of time and develop more complex pieces. Word study moves from phonic analysis to structural analysis, looking at word parts and patterns in word structures rather than only letters and letter sounds. Vocabulary study changes to include meaning of derivational roots and affixes as well as using context to determine word meaning. The use of resources, such as dictionaries and thesauruses, grows as children grow in their abilities to alphabetize and search texts quickly.

Figure 1.3   Instructional Tools for Literacy Development

	Early Elementary	*Transitional*	*Intermediate*
Reading	• Read aloud • Shared reading • Small-group guided reading in leveled texts with independent activities • Sharing	• Read aloud • Literature discussion groups based on read aloud • Reading minilesson • Shared reading • Small-group guided reading in leveled texts with independent activities, reading, and reading response • Sharing	• Reading minilesson • Book talks • Read aloud • Small-group guided reading or literature discussion groups • Independent reading and reading response • Sharing
Writing	• Minilesson • Independent writing and conferring • Small-group guided writing • Shared writing • Interactive writing • Sharing	• Minilesson • Independent writing and conferring • Small-group guided or interactive writing • Shared writing • Sharing	• Minilesson • Independent writing and conferring • Sharing
Word Study	• Oral language development • Phonemic awareness • Phonics minilesson • Spelling • Vocabulary development • Handwriting • Sharing	• Phonics minilesson • Word study minilesson • Spelling • Vocabulary development • Handwriting • Sharing	• Word study minilesson • Spelling • Vocabulary development • Handwriting • Sharing

REFLECTION

As we think about how children change as readers and writers and the kinds of instructional support they need, we feel a primary instructional focus may not fully meet the needs of children in Grades 2 and 3. This book represents our current thinking related to ways we can help primary children transition so they are better prepared to move into the challenges and demands of the intermediate grades. In addition to using what we know about literacy learning and teaching, we drew upon countless hours observing children and teachers at work in their classrooms in order to develop a better understanding of this process. We know there are many ways to support learners as they make this transition. Our hope is that some of the ideas included here will spur your thinking and lead you to reflect, question, and further develop your own teaching. This book is an invitation for you to join us as we continue to learn more about supporting children to grow as readers and writers.

2

Assessment

"**W**here do I begin? How do I know what they need and what they already know?" Most teachers start the year with the current book on standards and indicators for the state, the latest yearlong curriculum map for the appropriate grade level in a 3-inch binder, a folder with some text reading levels from last spring, and no information on several students who have come from other schools and districts. They often have samples of many of the students' writing from the end of the last year, along with writing-rubric scores from the previous year's assessment required by the district. Many teachers are overwhelmed by all this information and struggle to find a starting place that meets state and district requirements as well as the needs of their incoming students. As the year progresses, even more assessments are needed to monitor student progress, report achievement, and inform day-to-day teaching.

In this chapter, we discuss both formal and informal assessments for reading, writing, and word study and focus on those that are most appropriate for children moving from the primary to the intermediate grades. It is critical to understand children's strengths and needs as readers and writers in order to plan the most effective instruction for the whole class, small groups of children with similar needs, and individuals with unique needs.

There are a variety of purposes for assessing students and many ways in which to do so. Currently, there is an emphasis on assessment that uses the formal, standardized tests designed for high-stakes decision making through state initiatives and the No Child Left Behind Act of 2001. National and state academic content standards are assessed through norm-referenced and/or criterion-referenced forms of assessment designed to measure student achievement related to the standards. Tests are also used to determine continuous improvement as well as compare students from other districts, states, regions, and nations. Schools use these data to summarize achievement within and across classrooms and grade levels. These assessments typically include national, state, and district standardized tests.

Another use of assessment is to document progress for parents and students. This focuses on testing the students' understanding related to the specific curriculum being taught in various content areas in the classroom. It samples the kinds of knowledge gained over the course of the year. Many districts use annual, biannual, or quarterly assessments, such as writing rubrics and measures of text reading levels, to determine achievement. Even with all of these assessments, they may not provide enough information for teachers to use to inform their day-to-day instruction. Often, the information given is in the form of whether or not a child has met a passing score and does not guide teachers in how to teach the child the skills and strategies he or she needs. What is most important to teachers, and often gets neglected, is the use of assessment to understand what the children in the class know and are able to do. This is the ongoing, day-to-day, in-the-classroom assessment that provides information on the progress students are making as well as what they understand. It is the data used for making instructional decisions. The informal assessments in Figure 2.1 include things such as interviews; close observation of children during their independent work time (documented by written, dated anecdotal notes kept as records); performances of work in progress as well as completed work; students' daily, weekly, and end-of-unit artifacts and projects; and students' quality and levels of participation and engagement. Both formal and informal assessments guide instruction and evaluate learning. These are the types of assessments we address in the remainder of this chapter.

For children who will be facing heavy demands as readers and writers, it is critical to know their strengths, areas for growth, and interests. The data collected from day-to-day assessments inform and guide teachers as to the

Figure 2.1 Forms of Assessment

Formal Assessments: Assessments that have a standard form of measurement used to compare performance between students and for one student over time	Informal Assessments: Assessments that are based on the professional trained judgment of the teacher in determining the ongoing gains, progress, or needs of the student
• Final projects • Tests • Rubrics • Inventories • Running records • Reading level • Achievement tests • Norm-referenced, criterion-referenced, standardized, and/or performance-based assessments required at school, district, and/or state levels	• Interviews • Conversations (with students and parents) • Surveys (with students and parents) • Observations • Conferences • Performances • Reflections • Self-evaluations • On-the-spot evaluation integrated with teaching

most effective instructional decisions for individuals, small groups of children, and the whole class. While the curriculum provides an overview for the yearlong instructional journey with students, ongoing assessments indicate how long to spend at a certain location in the curriculum, when and which students are ready to move on or go back and review, whether something is already understood, and what path or direction to take through the curriculum. Questions teachers may have include the following: Where do I focus my whole-class instruction? Is it time to provide more or less instructional support in a given area? Is it time to move on to the next level, topic, or focus? For which learning goals do I need to teach students individually or in small groups? How will I effectively address students with special needs who are included in my classroom? Such questions are answered and become embedded in the instructional decisions that emerge from ongoing assessments.

While it may not seem easy to answer these questions, we want to share our thinking and provide possible approaches for effectively using assessment to guide instruction for transitional readers and writers. The most effective learning takes place not through delivering a predetermined curriculum, but rather through shifting, adjusting, and matching a curriculum to the needs of students, using thoughtful, effective, powerful instruction. Basing instructional decisions on information collected from both formal and informal assessments helps to maintain a close match between what students are ready to learn and how we might proceed with our teaching.

Children who are learning and functioning in a complex classroom setting have many differences. It is through close observation and assessment that we gain the most information about them. When we are puzzled about what to teach and how to teach it, assessing children can aid in clearing our confusions. What children independently say and do when we are not engaged in assisting and guiding them is the most powerful indicator of what is truly known and under their control. We must know our students, their strengths, and motives for learning, as well as their challenges. We must also know our curriculum, the big picture of where we're headed, and what it is we plan to accomplish. And we must know how to teach, how to touch the life of each child in our classrooms through teachable moments across the day, always following their leads and interests over the course of the year. This means helping children make connections between what they know and what we want them to learn, so they see themselves constantly discovering and learning.

To show progress, it is important to have a continuum against which to compare and note learning. There is both power and necessity for a curriculum as a way to chart a path for learning. The curriculum provides points of reference and helps determine areas for instruction based on the current strengths and understandings of each child. In addition to the informal assessments we use to guide instructional decisions, we also need formal assessments of reading and writing at key points of the year. This allows for an opportunity to note the range and progress of students over time and to determine whether some children are not making suitable progress and need additional instruction or support.

GETTING STARTED

During the first few weeks of school, we begin to establish a sense of classroom community and practice learning routines and expectations. As we engage in the process of getting to know one another, we waste no time gathering as much data as possible about each student's abilities and personal interests. This often includes a brief survey completed by parents on their views of their own children as learners and their children's interests, as well as information from parents related to goals and expectations they have for their children for the school year. We find this to be useful information when making decisions about instruction for specific students. It also provides a great place to begin conversations and conferences with parents throughout the year, but especially in our first one or two contacts. Figure 2.2 provides an example of a parent survey designed to provide information about the students' interests and reading and writing habits at home.

Figure 2.2   Family Letter

GETTING TO KNOW YOUR CHILD

Dear Families,

I am looking forward to working with your child this year! Because I appreciate all you do to support your child's education, I want to know more about him [or her] to help me plan for instruction. Please take a few minutes to answer the questions below and return this form to school.

Thank you.

1. How does your child use free time at home?

2. What do you enjoy doing together?

3. What are your child's strengths as a learner?

4. What does your child read at home?

5. What does your child write at home?

6. What do you read and write at home?

7. What goals do you have for your child this year?

8. What else would you like me to know about your child?

We also find it valuable to assess student interests and attitudes toward reading and writing. By the time children reach second and third grade, they have developed specific interests. Once we know those interests, we can build on them to motivate children to read and write. For example, students this age often get excited about series books like *Henry and Mudge* (e.g., Rylant, 1987) or *Magic Tree House* (e.g., Osborne, 1993). They are also interested in activities such as sports, dance classes, animals, video games, and collecting. An interest inventory can help teachers obtain this information. As part of an interest inventory, it is also useful to find out about students' attitudes and views toward reading and writing, through questions such as "What makes a good reader?" or "What do you need to do to be a better writer?" Responses such as "A good reader reads fast" or "A good reader gets all the words right" can lead to instruction on problem solving as a reader, expressive reading, and the importance of changing the rate for different reading purposes. Attitude surveys like the Elementary Reading Attitude Survey (McKenna & Kear, 1990) and the Writing Attitude Survey (Kear, Coffman, McKenna, & Ambrosio, 2000) can tell us whether we need to work on developing more positive attitudes toward reading and writing.

WORD STUDY

In addition to learning about student interests and attitudes to help motivate them to read and write, we also want to assess students on the central elements of reading: phonemic awareness, phonics, fluency, vocabulary, and comprehension (National Institute of Child Health and Human Development [NICHHD], 2001). Thus students' phonics, spelling, and word knowledge are assessed to plan instruction to meet the individual needs of all students. Most transitional readers in second and third grade no longer need assessment and instruction in phonemic awareness (Armbruster, Lehr, & Osborn, 2001). However, there may still be some struggling learners who need assessment in phonemic awareness in order to determine the direction for further instruction. Several subtests in Clay's *Observation Survey* (2002), such as hearing and recording sounds in words, word writing, and letter identification, could be used to assess struggling readers.

For most second graders, word study assessments focus on complex vowel and consonant patterns, decoding multisyllabic words, spelling high-frequency words, and the visual and meaning-based principles applied to spelling. Students' oral reading miscues can also be analyzed to determine how students work through words while reading extended text. Spelling error analysis inventories can be used to assess children's spelling and use of phonics knowledge in writing (Bear, Invernizzi, Templeton, & Johnston, 2003; Pinnell & Fountas, 1998).

Error analyses can be formal or informal. An example of an informal error analysis has the teacher list errors from children's independent writing and coding the errors onto a class record sheet. The Elementary Spelling Inventory (Bear et al., 2003) is a formal error analysis, with carefully selected lists of words that children write, similar to a traditional spelling test. However, the teacher notes which sounds and word features each child correctly represents in order to determine a developmental stage of spelling. This more formal error analysis includes common developmental spelling patterns. The Elementary Spelling Inventory is given to the entire class at one time and takes no more than 15 minutes to administer. It provides ways to differentiate during the assessment between more and less proficient spellers and categorizes students by developmental spelling stage. Each child's errors are coded and analyzed, and a class grid is developed to show error patterns across all students in the class. Once this is accomplished, the amount of critical information about spelling strategies being used by individual children and the class as a whole is remarkable. It is well worth the time spent to analyze this information, as it makes instructional decisions obvious and a teacher can plan for many weeks of instruction based on the errors. Using the error analysis assessments, instruction in word study, phonics, and spelling is based on the needs of the students. Combining this knowledge with the grade-level curriculum enables teachers to know where their students are in relation to state and district expectations. This allows for differentiation and acceleration for struggling learners as well as for those who are more capable or proficient learners.

READING

In addition to these aspects of word knowledge, we need to determine reading levels to set a benchmark for progress throughout the year and also to determine student strengths and areas for improvement through the analysis of oral reading and comprehension. If we're fortunate, we might have information on the level of text the child was reading in a guided-reading group from the previous year. This may include a running record (Clay, 2002) or miscue analysis (Wilde, 2000) that we can use to determine strengths in reading processing and areas for growth. Both running records and miscue analyses allow for coding of errors and opportunities for the teacher to analyze what the child is doing while problem solving during reading. For those children whose information is not available, we create time in the first few days of school to personally assess their text reading levels and analyze their reading. We attempt to assess at least one or two children each day, until we know reading levels for all the children and have a good idea of how they are processing text. Analyzing the problem-solving strategies a student uses when encountering difficulty while reading is a necessary part of being able to use assessment to inform instruction. Within days of beginning school, we can organize and begin direct instruction in reading with the whole class through read alouds and shared reading, focusing on comprehending and processing strategies often needed by the majority of the class at the beginning of the year.

Once we have assessed all the students who had no information available, we take time to briefly listen to each child read orally while the rest of the class is engaged in independent reading. While many second and third graders are proficient processors of text, we want to be sure they are fluent, expressive readers who demonstrate comprehension through attending to punctuation as well as character voice and other prosodic features. We also want to catch any struggling readers early in the year so we can plan extra instruction to accelerate their reading. In addition, after silent reading, we want to determine, through systematic retelling and questioning, how each child comprehends a text at his or her instructional reading level. This can be done through a retelling, a series of questions, or a comprehension rubric. Commercial assessments are available for this benchmark assessment process, or teachers may choose books from the classroom collection that are at various levels. There are several assessment systems available (Beaver, 1997; DeFord, 2001), as well as resources for teachers to develop benchmark book sets from their classroom libraries (Fountas & Pinnell, 2006).

Once this information is collected, it should be reviewed and analyzed with a focus on instructional needs. For example, after analyzing reading assessments early in the year, Carla, a second-grade teacher, realized that her assessments indicated that most of the students struggled to retell stories they had easily read. This led her to plan several whole-group, shared-reading lessons designed to help the students in her class learn what to include when retelling a story and to practice doing it in a highly supportive context. With her whole-group focus determined, Carla turned her attention to the needs of specific students. Using running-record information, she did an initial grouping of the children for reading instruction, based on text level. Upon closer examination of one child's reading, she noted that he was able to use meaning along with visual word analysis to solve most unknown words; however, he struggled with words with more than one syllable. Observation and analysis of other students' reading revealed that four additional children had similar difficulty. Though not all of these children were at the same text level, Carla decided to group them for instruction aimed at this specific skill.

WRITING

Using writing assessment to make instructional decisions takes a similar form. From the previous year, we may have rubric scores for end-of-year writing performances. A variety of writing rubrics are available, and many school districts have created their own. Most writing rubrics rate individual students' abilities to organize their writing, stick to a topic, add detail and interesting words, and use conventions such as spelling and punctuation. While this information is useful, we also suggest collecting an independent writing sample from each child in the first weeks of school. This can be a whole-group activity, using a prompt and providing about 30 minutes of independent writing time. During this time, we observe and take anecdotal notes on individual students' levels of engagement during writing and how students use the resources in the classroom. We also record when, how, and to whom we provide assistance. Our initial writing minilessons will focus on some of the observed issues. Over the next week, we analyze the children's writing and chart strengths and needs of individuals in order to determine whole-class, small-group, and individual instruction in writing. In Figure 2.3, the teacher created just such a chart to focus on two aspects of craft, organization and topic focus, to determine how students were doing in these areas and what needed to be taught next. Figure 2.3 is a portion of a teacher's class chart as an example that will be discussed in more detail in Chapter 5.

Figure 2.3   Example of Class Analysis Grid

	Well Organized	Is Focused on Topic		
Meredith	X	X		
Kareem	X	X		
Helena	X	X		
Anita	X			
Korey				
Alex	X			
Melissa	X			
Rachel		X		
Ruth	X	X		
Jana	X	X		
Stefanie	X	X		
Bryan				
José	X			
Quinton	X	X		
Blaze	X			
Jasmine		X		
Robin	X			
Yahira		X		
Dawn	X			
Lisa	X	X		
Carmen	X			
Aminah	X	X		
Mitchell	X			
Hiram	X			

Often, additional assessments need to be given at the beginning of the school year to meet requirements for the district-level testing. If these assessments provide meaningful information we can use for instruction, we can use the information collected for the district as a place to begin teaching. If not, we complete the district data collection as required but move forward with instruction based on data we've personally collected on these students.

Anecdotal Notes

Over the course of the year, we try to record anecdotal notes monthly on each student in the class, with a focus on their skills, strategies, and behaviors in both reading and writing. For students who struggle, we attempt to observe more often and collect weekly notes during times of independent reading and writing or during small-group guided reading and writing. It is extremely important for us to understand the needs of struggling learners, because they are easily confused and need clear direction and additional support for success. Anecdotal notes often refer to something observed as the child works independently to practice and apply new learning. We may be noticing whether students are applying a teaching point we made in a one-on-one instructional moment. Or we could be recording an observation of a child's progress toward a goal established between the child and the teacher related to a change in behavior or attitude. Anecdotal notes provide a written record of anything important in the moment and allow for more thought and reflection on student progress at a time when we are not directly engaged with whole-class instruction of students. Some helpful questions to ask and then record your thoughts on during observations are as follows: How long is the child on task when doing independent work? What is he or she doing in relation to the assigned task? What are his or her reading or writing behaviors when working without teacher support? Figure 2.4 shows some examples of anecdotal notes recorded by Marcia, a third-grade teacher, while observing a child reading independently.

The organization of taking and collecting anecdotal records is probably the most challenging aspect of the assessment process. We've tried several ways, and all have their advantages and disadvantages. Sheets with boxes or lines and names prerecorded make it easy to collect the data while moving around the classroom but may be more difficult to work with during the time set aside for reflecting on progress of individual students. Sheets on individual students are cumbersome for some teachers when taking notes in the context of the classroom but are wonderful at the time of reflection, since all comments for one student are dated and on one single sheet. One teacher commented on her procedure and said, "I just pull papers for kids I know I want to see and put them on top of my stack and work my way through them in order over the course of the day. Any others I see that day are a bonus."

Another method that works well for some teachers is to use sheets of labels that have been run on a computer merge program to place a student's name on each label. Each student has one label on a single sheet of paper, and teachers can take notes on each student's label when observing children in the class. At the end of the week, the labels can be peeled from the single sheet and placed in each individual child's folder for easy reflection at a later time.

Another method is to organize a clipboard as a portable flip chart. On the clipboard are large note cards, each with a child's name written on a lower corner. These are taped overlapping and alphabetically down the clipboard so all names are visible to allow the teacher to quickly flip to the

Figure 2.4 Samples of Anecdotal Notes

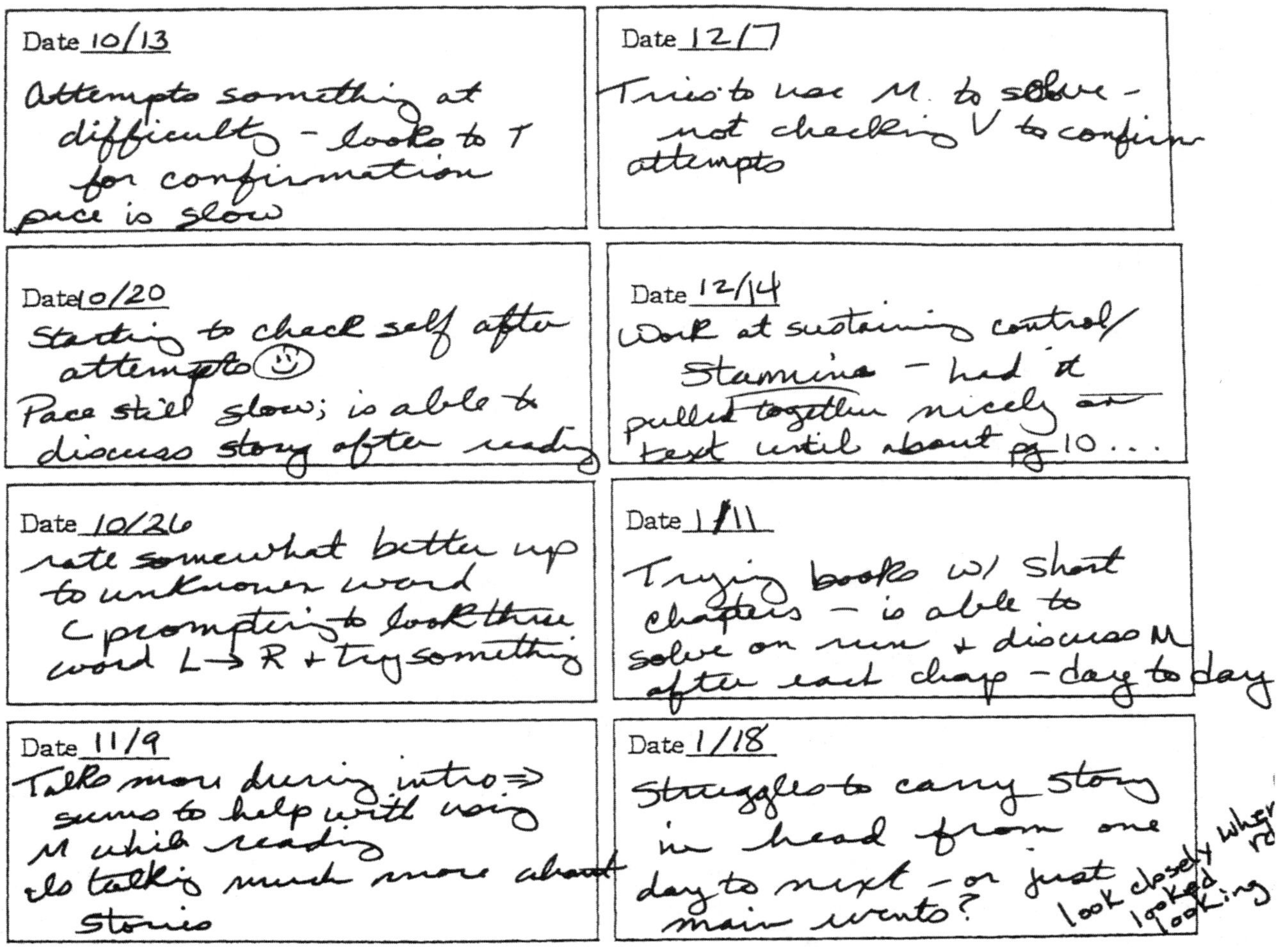

Date 10/13
Attempts something at difficulty - looks to T for confirmation pace is slow

Date 12/7
Tries to use M. to solve - not checking V to confirm attempts

Date 10/20
Starting to check self after attempts ☺
Pace still slow; is able to discuss story after reading

Date 12/14
Work at sustaining control/ Stamina - had it pulled together nicely on text until about pg 10 . . .

Date 10/26
rate somewhat better up to unknown word c prompting to look thru word L → R + try something

Date 1/11
Trying books w/ short chapters - is able to solve on run + discuss M after each chap - day to day

Date 11/9
Talks more during intro ⇒ seems to help with using M while reading
Is talking much more about stories

Date 1/18
struggles to carry story in head from one day to next - or just main events?
look closely when looking

card of the student being observed. All students' cards are easily available on the clipboard and later, when the cards are filled, can be placed in their individual folders.

Scheduling specific times during independent reading and writing to routinely watch and listen to students engaged in independent work helps to clarify what is really known and being applied by students independent of teacher support. Then, by taking the time each week to quickly review the anecdotal records, teachers get a sense of what students are applying or not applying while reading and writing. In addition, this information can indicate needs for whole-group minilessons or small-group instruction.

As a regular practice, Greg, a third-grade teacher, takes about 15 minutes each week to scan his notes, jotting ideas for minilessons or names of children who could be grouped for a specific lesson. While it is necessary to take a more detailed look at notes from time to time, these quick looks are more realistic on a weekly basis. In addition, Greg makes sure to spend time looking more closely at the notes he took while observing the students who are struggling. Children who are having difficulty need close monitoring in order to plan instruction that can accelerate their learning.

Running Records

Along with the observations and anecdotal records being compiled in individual students' folders, regular running records on reading performance should be taken and analyzed every week for students we are worried about. While regular running records are important for younger children who are learning to process text, more proficient readers in second and third grade will often read with such accuracy that there are few errors to analyze. Students reading at higher text levels show evidence they are using strategies and sources of information even when they continue to make errors. Completing running records as part of a benchmarking process at each marking period can be sufficient for students who are making good progress as readers. Running records on longer texts need be taken on only approximately 100 words of continuous text and not on the entire piece. This saves time and yields enough information for making instructional decisions. In addition to formal running records, taking notes on errors observed at the guided-reading table and in reading conferences also informs instruction.

Conference Notes

Writing samples can be collected and analyzed two or three times a quarter by using a writing rubric or by analyzing for specific concerns. However, information is also gathered during writing conferences on a more routine basis. When planning for a writing conference, teachers review notes taken and goals set at previous conferences and use that information to guide instruction in the current conference.

Figure 2.5 shows a simple chart that Shandra, a second-grade teacher, used during writing. As Shandra conferred with Lindsey, she guided the student to choose a goal that would help her become a better writer. As they looked back over recent work each time they conferred, they gained evidence to help them develop a goal for Lindsey to work on. Shandra wrote the goal in language Lindsey could understand. In each conference, they reviewed the most recent goal and looked for evidence that Lindsey was meeting this goal in her current writing. Lindsey chose to use smiley faces to indicate that her goals were being successfully met. After two or three smiley faces across the columns, it was evident that the usage was solidly in place, and a new goal was determined. Though very basic in nature, this system helped Lindsey begin to take more responsibility for learning and increase her own awareness of progress toward goals.

Figure 2.5   Personal Writing Goals for One Child

My Goals as a Writer

Date	Goal			
12-2	Add an ending sentence to my stories	:-	:)	:)
1-4	Use words that make a picture (close my eyes, think, write)	:)	:)	
1-23	Find where most of the periods go in my story. read it out loud!	:-	:-	:)
2-2	Try out other types of writing	:)		

USING ASSESSMENT

One caveat that needs to be mentioned is the importance of taking time to assess and observe students' independent work. We need to make sure that students are applying their learning when reading and writing on their own and demonstrating that they can use what they are learning independently and flexibly. For example, if students have learned the word study principle of looking for parts they know to decode a new word and we have evidence they can do this with pairs of words in isolation, we also want to see them apply this to new words when reading and writing. It takes both formal and informal data in a variety of settings to be sure a student has learned to use their knowledge independently in a range of situations. If we see that learning is not transferring to different independent contexts, we need to reteach that strategy in a new way.

Any time there is a question or concern about a child in the classroom, some form of data should be collected to help answer the question. The chart in Figure 2.6 provides an overview of the collection of data. This can be useful in planning for student assessment throughout the school year. In addition to how data collection might look across the year, it is important to keep in mind the view that assessment leads to instructional decisions about what to teach and when and how to teach it. Students are central to this process. Teachers just don't "do" assessment to students. By second grade, teachers can work with students to set short- and long-term goals based on assessment results. Students and teachers should meet together during reading and writing conferences to set clear, specific goals. The beauty of

Figure 2.6 Overview of Assessment Collection

Assessments	Reading	Writing	Word Study
Yearly Assessments	• Benchmark assessment • National, state, or district achievement tests	• National, state, or district achievement tests	• National, state, or district achievement tests
Quarterly Assessments	• Running records on high-achieving students • District tests	• Writing rubric on random sample • District writing prompt	• Spelling inventory • District tests
Monthly Assessments	• Running records for average students	• Informal checklist on random samples	• Error analysis on random writing samples
Assessments done every 1 to 2 weeks	• Running records on low-achieving students • Guided reading/conferring notes	• Conferring notes	• Weekly spelling tests • Notes on decoding/writing errors of lowest-progress students

using assessment to establish individual goals is that the teacher has so much information about the student that all goals are well within the student's ability to achieve. In addition, during future conferences, there are opportunities for students to monitor their own growth as they are taught how to set personal learning goals and assess their own progress in reaching them.

FINDING TIME

While teachers agree that assessing students is important, we know that finding time to do it is not so easy. Having a plan, perhaps following the overview in Figure 2.6, can help teachers manage time for assessments. Though standardized assessments and unit tests may be administered to whole groups at one time, many of the informal assessments that are useful for informing instruction need to be done in small groups or with individuals. We have found that some assessments can become part of the instructional routine. For example, anecdotal notes can be completed as the teacher is conferring with an individual while the other children are reading and writing independently. Running records can be taken with one child at the start of a guided-reading lesson while the rest of the group is rereading texts for fluency practice. Periodically, the time usually spent conducting guided-reading groups or conferring with writers may be set aside in order to assess students. Since students are comfortable working independently during those times, the teacher does not have to worry about what the rest of the class will do while she briefly works with a small group or individual students.

REFLECTION

To function as professional educators, we must know the strengths students bring to our classroom more than we need to know their age and grade levels. This means watching, listening, talking with, and professionally assessing them from the moment they enter our classroom community. Assessment enables us to find ways to connect with each student and to find out who they are as individuals and what they bring as learners into our classroom communities. Ongoing assessment allows us to ensure that teaching the child is our instructional priority. This includes helping children become problem solvers rather than "grade-getters" and "teacher-pleasers" (Johnston, 2004). Johnston suggests that we use the language of assessment as a continual spiral between instruction and learning. When we know where students are as readers, writers, word solvers, and spellers and we know the curriculum and where we're headed, we can plan the actual instruction to meet the specific needs of each of our students. We all recognize that each student will carve his or her own path through the curricular continuum. We can help chart that path by the explicit language we use when we teach with assessment in mind. We can say to students, "I noticed in your work . . ." or "I noticed while you were working . . . ." This provides students with the idea that they should be noticing things in their own work, and it gives them a rationale for the instruction that will follow.

Our next explicit teaching move would be to say, "Today we will learn to . . ." and then model, demonstrate, and talk through the process we want students to be able to do. Finally, framing the lesson with the words, "So, when you read today, try this. . . ." provides specific expectations for students to practice their new learning independently and across different contexts. Through an immediate link between assessment and teaching, we ensure that students will have the best chance of knowing what to do with the instruction they receive.

In the coming chapters, we base our thoughts on instruction for learners in transition on routine informal as well as formal assessment, while keeping in mind curricular demands. Through careful and systematic use of assessment, we are able to make more powerful instructional decisions and focus our teaching on the strengths and needs of each individual student.

3

Word Study

On a January day in Megan's second-grade classroom, she closely observed some children in one of her reading groups as they read a book, noting that they seemed to be more capable today at solving complex words without prompts from her. She checked on their most recent running records and noticed they had typically attempted unknown words using only the first letter instead of looking all the way through the word. As a result, her teaching points over the past week had centered on teaching this group to look carefully through words sequentially, from left to right, blending sounds while using the visual information available to them. Although the behaviors of the students today indicated they were successfully taking on this skill, Megan was curious as to the extent to which these young readers realized and could articulate what they were doing. As they finished reading, Megan said, "Wow! Today you really seemed to know how to handle tricky words while you were reading. What was happening as you read?"

Drake leaned forward and earnestly explained, "Well, I just learned that when you read, you have to be careful of the vowels and the consequences!" Though shaky in his use of terms, Drake was indicating a sense that he could apply what he was learning about letters, sounds, and words to help him while reading.

In our work in many schools, we found numerous examples of teachers who believed students were "getting it" during word study instruction but not connecting what they could do during word study to their reading and writing. As classroom teachers, we know only too well the ongoing issue of students successfully passing the Friday spelling test only to have those very same words misspelled in written work or not recognized during text reading. In much the same manner, we spend instructional time ensuring that students can recite various phonics rules, and we provide time for practice and successful application during assessment, yet we often see little carry-over into the real work of reading and writing. Many children seem to view word study lessons as completely separate from reading and writing. They may not realize that the purpose for learning about sounds and words is to help them decode words when reading and construct words when writing. In addition, transitional learners need to become successful, flexible, and efficient when decoding and constructing words. Being able to solve new words quickly makes it much easier for young readers and writers to handle longer and more complex texts.

In this chapter, we explore the shifts word learners make and how thoughtful instruction can support these shifts. We define the areas of word study most appropriate for children in transition as phonological awareness, phonics, structural analysis, high-frequency words, and vocabulary development. This includes suggestions for ways teachers might link word study to support the real work of reading and writing.

In our experience, most children eagerly join in when provided opportunities for meaningful activities centered on words and how they work. Activities such as generating lists, breaking apart or building words, sorting, and searching for patterns help us realize that there is an endless list of possible ways to explore letters, sounds, and words. Though this playful exploration may seem more appropriate in the early primary classrooms, Booth (1999) believes that "word play is a legitimate and valuable classroom activity even after children have become readers and writers. It helps children consciously examine oral and written language while they learn to manipulate and control it" (p. 91). Learners in transition continue to need many opportunities to manipulate letters, sounds, and words in a variety of ways.

Since children benefit from focused work with letters and words and how they work, our goal is to connect this learning to reading and writing in extended texts.

> Children are quite willing to take small detours—learning words and how they work, hearing and recording sounds while constructing messages, or analyzing words while reading—if these activities are in the service of real reading and writing. (Fountas & Pinnell, 1996, p. 13)

To know how to help students use what they have learned, it is important to understand how learners in transition shift in terms of their knowledge of letters, sounds, and words. If we look at word study as an isolated event, separate from text reading and writing, it may appear that learners in transition quickly move toward independence as word solvers. However, many of these learners need high levels of support in understanding how to apply their knowledge about words to help in the act of reading and writing. Explicit teaching in this area is necessary. But even more important is to structure time for students to experience contexts that vary in the amount of teacher support and allow for differentiation based on learners' needs. Students need multiple experiences to build networks for understanding. These experiences must include various amounts of teacher and peer support to meet the diverse needs of learners in the classroom. We can support students in a variety of ways:

- Consistent routines for word study
- Minilessons that provide explicit models and demonstrations
- Whole-group, small-group, and individual practice activities
- Opportunities for sorting and manipulating letters, sounds, and words
- Links to real reading and writing through shared reading and interactive writing
- Time to articulate and share new understandings and application of new knowledge
- Word walls and charts for various collections of words

The different instructional contexts listed above provide for the gradual release of responsibility from direct word study lessons to application in reading and writing.

These supports are embedded throughout this chapter as we discuss the needs of transitional learners and how word study instruction can meet their needs. Using these supports enables teachers to provide powerful instruction, while continually adjusting the level of support provided to students. The primary goal is to ensure not only that students learn important concepts about letters, sounds, and words but also that they will make use of this knowledge while reading and writing.

Almost any activity can be used with varied levels of support. For example, a teacher might demonstrate, by providing a high level of support to students, how she groups words when sorting by initial letter. As students become more capable, she might ask them to join in, making the sorting a shared experience, with the children helping to decide which words to place in each category. When the students are ready, the task might move to a literacy station or become an independent activity, both of which offer low levels of teacher support. The key to knowing when to shift instructional contexts comes from what we learn about students' understandings and applications through the analysis of assessments and observations. At the same time, it is also important for us to understand how children change as readers and writers as they move toward intermediate grades. Figure 3.1 outlines some of the changes children make in word study during these years.

LEARNING ABOUT WORDS

What is it like to learn words and learn about how words work during a time of major transition in the primary grades? Let's first take a look at what one student learned as a foundation prior to the time of transition. As an entry-level primary student, Luis had many experiences with letters, sounds, and words. At first, his understanding of what words look like and how to read and write them was limited to an emphasis on his name and the names of

Figure 3.1 Change Over Time in Word Knowledge

Word Study	• Has basic knowledge of letter/sound relationships • Knows consonants, blends short- and long-vowel patterns in single-syllable words • Uses sound analysis when spelling unknown words • Has a basic writing vocabulary of some high-frequency words • Uses basic vocabulary to express thoughts	• Has knowledge of consonant clusters, more complex visual vowel patterns to represent sounds • Uses inflectional endings, simple suffixes, and compound words • Knows many high-frequency words • Uses sound analysis for spelling unknown words and begins to use visual analysis • Uses more precise vocabulary	• Has basic phonics under control • Understands structural analysis of words, including affixes, root and base words, and multisyllable words • Has high-frequency words under control in both reading and writing tasks • Uses visual analysis and understanding of word structure in spelling • Refines and extends vocabulary

his classmates. From the visual recognition of letter clusters and patterns in names, he extended his focus to sounds and letter/sound representations. As Luis progressed, he also started focusing attention on high-frequency words found in simple books and poems. Luis entered first grade with a group of 10 to 40 well-known words he could both read and write accurately. His list included, but was not limited to, his first and last name, the first names of his brothers and sisters, the words *mom* and *dad*, names of pets, and a few high-frequency words, such as *I, a, the, see, like, go, no, me, can, to, my, we, love,* and *you.* Though the words Luis knew at the end of the year were not all the same as those of his classmates, everyone had a set of core words they were able to use as anchors for both reading and writing of simple text.

Luis also spent a lot of time early in his school career engaging with the sounds of language. Activities such as songs, chants, and picture sorts helped him develop phonological awareness. He and most of his classmates learned to listen for and distinguish between beginning and ending sounds of words. By the end of the year, these students were discerning sounds in the middle of words as well. Learning to attach the letter symbols to sounds was the focus of Luis's early experiences with phonics. Specifically, he was learning to connect visual symbols to the sounds for consonants, blends, and short vowels. Over the course of his primary experience, he also showed an emerging knowledge of long-vowel patterns in single-syllable words. While writing, Luis used sound analysis for spelling unknown words ("uv" for *of,* "chruk" or "jruk" for *truck,* etc.). In both written and oral expression, he used basic vocabulary to express his thoughts.

As a first grader, Luis used his initial pool of 10 to 40 words to build a larger and more complex pool of words, ranging from 100 to 250 words, that he could recognize and use flexibly in reading and writing. This was accomplished through a variety of reading, writing, and word study activities. At this stage, Luis and his classmates extended their working knowledge of words and spelling by building families of words (e.g., *can, ran, man, fan,*

Dan; hand, land, sand; book, look, took, etc.). They also wrote new words through careful articulation and recording of sounds they were able hear when attempting to write an unknown word. They typically used consonants correctly but often struggled to accurately record vowels.

Now in the transitional phase between primary and intermediate grades, Luis has moved from building a consistently reliable system for learning words and how they work to a time of noticing various visual patterns used to create the same sounds. One example is all the different visual spelling patterns that provide the "long a" sound in English ("ai" in *train,* "ay" in *day,* "a consonant e" in *late,* "ei" in *vein,* "eigh" in *eight*). One critical shift Luis needed to make in his learning was moving from a reliance on simple letter-sound relationships to a focus on a variety of patterns for single sounds in spelling. Luis's knowledge of sound-symbol relationships has grown to include consonant clusters and more complex vowel patterns. He uses inflectional endings, such as "ing" and "ed." In addition, Luis has learned about categories of words, such as compound words, contractions, and homophones. He uses sound analysis combined with visual patterns more effectively for spelling unknown words and has begun to use visual analysis when decoding multisyllable words in reading. Luis's vocabulary has increased with exposure to new concepts, and he uses more precise language for concepts he already has under control. Instead of using simple language, like *walk,* Luis is beginning to use vocabulary such as *saunter, glide,* or *drift,* all of which are more precise than words he used as an early primary student. The core of high-frequency words Luis can read and write continues to grow rapidly, and he uses more precise vocabulary when expressing himself. In addition, Luis and his classmates are more efficient and flexible as they use their expanding knowledge about letters, sounds, and words when reading and writing.

Now that we know more about how one learner was changing as he moved from the primary to intermediate grades, we will take a closer look at how instruction can support children as they gain knowledge about words and how they work. This includes learning to use what they know while reading and writing independently. There are key elements of word study that are important during transition. Using these key elements of word study in Figure 3.2, we will share what we have learned about supporting learners in transition, using several instructional contexts. This allows us to build on student strengths by providing instruction that meets them on the edge of their learning, moving them toward independence.

PHONOLOGICAL AND PHONEMIC AWARENESS

One area we know is critical for learning to become literate in the early years is *phonological awareness.* If children are to attach letter symbols to the sounds of language, it helps if they are able to hear the sounds that make up words (Booth, 1999). While the basic ability to blend and segment speech sounds is in place for most students by second grade (Armbruster, Lehr, & Osborn,

Figure 3.2   Key Elements for Word Study

Phonological Awareness	*Phonological awareness* is general understanding that speech is made up of different sounds and patterns. Phonological awareness includes recognizing rhymes and syllables as well as blending and segmenting sounds, as in onsets and rimes in words. Phonemic awareness is part of phonological awareness.
Phonemic Awareness	*Phonemic awareness* is the ability to notice, think about, and work with sounds in oral language and how they work together to make words. It includes the ability to hear, identify, and manipulate the individual sounds of language. The smallest parts of oral language are called *phonemes.*
Phonics	*Phonics* is a method of teaching the relationship between the symbols and sounds of language and teaches the alphabetical principles of written language. Phonics connects phonemes with *graphemes*—the smallest parts of written language.
Structural Analysis	*Structural analysis* involves using word parts to understand meaning units within words. It is based on morphemes, the smallest units of meaning in words. This includes knowledge of root words, compound words, affixes, and syllabication.
High-Frequency Words	*High-frequency words* are words that are frequently encountered in reading and writing. Readers need to develop a core of known words in order to process text efficiently. The term *sight words* refers to words that are not phonetically regular or are beyond the current abilities of the reader to decode phonetically. What may be a sight word for a first-grade child may be within the decoding ability of a second grader, though still considered a high-frequency word (for example, *like*).
Vocabulary Development	*Vocabulary development* refers to the repertoire of words used or known by an individual or group. The words that make up a person's vocabulary range from general to specific. We often think of vocabulary study as helping children understand word meanings, but it could also refer to types of words (such as homophones, synonyms, etc.) as well as developing a richer language base.

2001), many learners in transition still need to refine their phonological and phonemic awareness. In particular, further instruction is needed in differentiating between short-vowel sounds and hearing all the sounds in consonant blends.

One of the most effective components of word study for developing *phonemic awareness* is the use of picture sorts. For example, Melissa's second-grade students started the year struggling to hear the difference between short-vowel sounds in single-syllable words. She used simple pictures of objects such as "bed," "hill," "cat," "top," and "rug" for whole-class demonstrations. For the first lesson, Melissa chose to use only pictures with the "short a" and "short i" sounds. She carefully said each word, making sure to not stretch the sounds unnaturally. After repeating the word several times to the class, she carefully placed the cards with pictures that had "short a" sounds on one side of a chart and those with "short i" on the other side. Melissa made sure to model exactly how to say the words before considering where to place them on the chart. She wanted her students to listen to the sounds of the words.

The next day, Melissa and the students repeated the lesson, but this time she invited the students to join her in saying the words and allowed them to decide which words belonged on which side of the chart. Sharing the activity through this guided practice, Melissa gradually turned over the task to students who were ready, while still guiding others as needed. After a few days, the activity was moved into the word study station, an area of the room where children could engage in activities independently to reinforce and extend their learning (Diller, 2003). The children were able to successfully sort pictures between the two short-vowel sounds on their own. Over the next few weeks, Melissa used the same technique to add pictures to the sort with all the short-vowel sounds. Later in the year, the class once again went back to sorting pictures using criteria such as comparing blends at the end of words and comparing words with long-vowel sounds to words with short-vowel sounds.

To help students develop strong phonological awareness, we can guide them during shared-reading activities to attend to onsets and rimes, rhyming words, and syllable junctures. Linking print to phonological awareness helps children see how they can use this knowledge as readers and writers and provides additional support to children who are still learning letters (Armbruster et al., 2001). Reading stories, poems, and chants together quickly builds a large collection of text with which students are familiar. Rereading those texts and listening for certain sounds can help sharpen phonological awareness. After one shared reading, Dianne highlighted the rhyming words from the book *The Cake That Jake Baked* (Hennessy, 1990) and listed the words on a class chart, noting the rime in each word. She often referred to this chart and similar charts to help children problem solve using a part from one of the known words to read or write an unfamiliar word, a strategy they would be able to access and apply later during their independent work time.

PHONICS

In addition to phonological awareness, students transitioning from primary to intermediate grades need to continue applying and extending their strategic processing and word analysis when reading and should become more effective at constructing a larger number of complex words. This shift goes beyond simple letter/sound relationships and means that children need to attend not only to how parts of words sound but also to how words look. For example, a child in primary grades might hear the "long e" sound in the word *eat* but record that sound with a single "e." Learners in transition are starting to notice that the "long e" sound is usually represented visually by one of several patterns (*eat, Pete, tree*). They also become aware of other spelling patterns that may not look like they sound, such as "ight" in *night* or "ph" in *phone.*

Much attention has been devoted to the teaching of phonics, and there are many commercial programs and methods available. According to the National Reading Panel (National Institute of Child Health and Human Development [NICHHD], 2001), systematic phonics instruction is critical in the development of reading. No matter which approach is being used, we have found a few key components to be particularly effective:

- Making sure children hear and differentiate the sounds being studied
- Teaching children to notice the visual patterns in words and ways the visual information relates to the sounds they hear
- Explicitly stating phonics principles and concepts in simple, clear language
- Teaching strategies that help children decide which pattern to use in a given word
- Deliberately connecting patterns being studied in isolation to word work in continuous text (decoding in reading and constructing in writing)

Before teaching children the visual patterns used to represent sounds, we first make sure they can hear and differentiate the sounds as part of the development of their phonological awareness. After students become proficient at hearing sounds, we can teach them to attend to visual patterns using word sorts. For example, when learning the sound /ou/, as in *out* or *flower,* Beth's second-grade students first sorted words into piles that had "ou" and piles with "ow." Later, they sorted by whether the letters representing the /ou/ sound were at the beginning, middle, or end of the words. This led some students to discover and predict that when they heard this particular sound at the end of a word, it would most likely be represented with the letters "ow," as in *cow.*

Though we guide students to notice word parts based on a set pattern or sound, there is value in using open sorts to allow children to determine a spelling principle, such as number of vowels, number of syllables, or words with "silent e," and so on. This encourages children to attend more closely to the visual aspects of words and notice similarities and differences in how words look and sound. Another type of sort is a *blind sort.* In this sort, one child reads the word on a card to another child, who then places it in a certain category without having seen the visual pattern in the word. Doing this makes children use what they hear to predict what they will see in a word. For example, if the word on the card is *pig,* the child who cannot see the card hears the short-vowel sound in the middle and must decide what letter is likely to represent that sound. We also occasionally have students participate in *speed sorts.* Children are asked to sort words in a limited amount of time, either using a spelling principle we have determined or one they choose to use. This forces students to quickly notice patterns and categorize the words. Learners in transition need to be able to quickly apply what they know about words when reading and writing, and activities such as this can help them learn to recognize and use patterns with more efficiency.

Helping transitional learners articulate what they are noticing about words is another key to effective phonics instruction. Often, the teacher may begin his or her instruction with a short, focused lesson, typically called a *minilesson,* stating a principle and demonstrating it to students. When Beth's students began to learn about consonant blends, she started her minilesson by stating the principle, "When two consonants are together in a word and you can hear the sounds for both letters together, it is called a 'consonant blend'" (Fountas & Pinnell, 2003). She wrote several words containing consonant blends on a chart, underlining the blends, such as *bl*ue, *st*op, and ha*nd.* Beth carefully said each word as she slid her finger under it, drawing attention to how the word sounded and looked. Later, students noticed that "th," "wh," and "ph" were different. They told Beth that when the letter "h" was after another consonant, it worked with that consonant to make a new sound. They wrote this observation at the top of a chart filled with these words. It is helpful for children to be able to name what they notice about words and how the English language works.

While direct, explicit instruction and sorts are critical in phonics instruction, our end goal is for students to use what they learn about letters and sounds when reading and writing extended texts. It is important in word study to include deliberate instruction in linking this isolated learning to the work of reading and writing. For example, during shared reading lessons, the teacher might mask the vowel in a word and have children think about what they already know about letters, sounds, and words to predict the letter or letters they could expect to see, followed by checking to confirm their predictions. After doing interactive or shared writing, the teacher might have the children work in pairs to apply their learning related to spelling patterns as they negotiate the decoding and construction of unknown words in text. This type of linking instruction with shared and guided practice will continue over time, with a clear expectation that what is practiced and learned during word study is to be used when reading and writing. As the sophistication of students' learning in word study increases, their ability to apply word patterns, strategies, and concepts should become more flexible and automatic.

An activity one teacher found useful for students helps them link their learning about letters and sounds to their independent reading. After learning patterns for the "long e" sound ("ea," "ee," and "e consonant e"), the class created a chart with lists of words containing each "long e" pattern. Later in the week, the teacher asked students to scan the books they had selected for independent reading that day. When they found a word with a "long e" pattern, they wrote it on a piece of scrap paper. After the students looked for several minutes, the teacher gathered the children near the chart containing lists of the words they had previously sorted and been using. The children shared the "long e" words they found in their books, adding them to the appropriate categories on the chart. The activity helped this teacher's students not only to notice these patterns in continuous text, but also to realize that learning the patterns would assist them when reading. As one student explained, "You sure were right. These sounds are in lots of books!"

In addition to decoding, understanding phonics principles helps learners in transition construct words while writing. Interactive writing is a powerful and effective way to do this. It involves a collaborative effort in composing and constructing a written text, with the teacher and the children sharing the pen (McCarrier, Pinnell, & Fountas, 1999). During interactive writing, the teacher and the children work together to compose and write a message. The teacher makes deliberate decisions about specific words in the message that lend themselves to model his or her teaching point. For example, if the children have been learning about words with long vowels, the teacher may choose to have the children help write those words. One child would come to the front to record the word on the chart paper, while the teacher would guide the rest of the children to decide which letters represent the long-vowel sound in that word. Other times, the teacher might ask the children what patterns could represent a certain sound, writing the word on a small dry-erase board, using each pattern *(teeth, teath)*. She would then ask the children which way "looks right," not only helping them review patterns that could reasonably make that sound but also modeling a visual strategy for deciding on the appropriate pattern (Cunningham, 1999; Routman, 1991).

Another way to reinforce the use of what is being learned during word study is to ask children to review their independent writing. They may list words in their own writing that follow a certain pattern or highlight those words in their first drafts. This continual linking of learning taking place during word study to real reading and writing is powerful and critical. When teachers notice that students are not applying what they know about words and how the words work, they can plan lessons to deliberately link word study to reading and writing tasks.

After noticing students were not using words they already knew to help them solve new words quickly when reading, Ruth planned a minilesson to review this strategy with her second graders. During word study that day, she used magnetic letters to show students the word *well*, which all of them knew. She reminded them they could change the first letter/sound of this word to make new words, such as *shell* and *tell*. Ruth continued to demonstrate how she could use this knowledge to quickly figure out an unknown word when reading. She used the sentence "The bump on his knee started to swell." When she got to the word *swell*, she paused and thought aloud, "Oh! This looks like well . . . /sw/-/ell/ . . . swell!" Ruth told students she had noticed when they were reading that they were not using this strategy to help them solve new words quickly and maintain reading momentum. In closing the lesson, she made sure students knew this was a strategy used by competent readers and one they could use in their own reading.

At the end of the day, Ruth found a book on her desk with a bookmark sticking out of the top. Opening to that page, she discovered this note from one of her students, shown in Figure 3.3.

The next day, Ruth used this student's note as a follow-up lesson, showing the other children how their classmate had applied the strategy. As a result, many more notes began to appear from other children who

Figure 3.3   Student's Letter

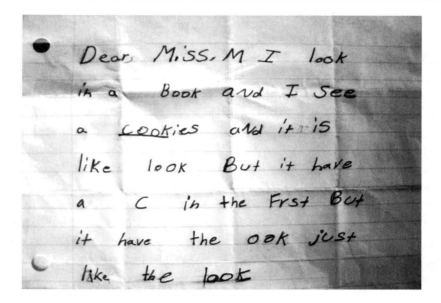

were attempting to apply what they had been taught. In guided-reading groups, several children made sure to apply the strategy overtly, first saying the known word, nodding to themselves, and then saying the new word so Ruth could "catch" them in the act of being a reader! The children quickly internalized the new strategy, and it became more difficult to detect as they applied it quickly and silently.

STRUCTURAL ANALYSIS

As transitional learners begin to notice more about word parts, the time is right to teach them about the structural aspects of words, such as contractions, inflectional endings, and possessives. Though they certainly have encountered contractions and words ending with "s" and "ing" before, they are now ready to understand how structure, meaning, and sounds of words may change.

Knowing when to use "s" or "es" can be tricky. After a lesson on what it means when "s" or "es" is added to a word, Lorena, a third-grade teacher, placed several cards with words such as *buses* and *balls* on a large pocket chart. She told the children to watch. She placed cards with words such as *buses, churches,* and *dishes* on one side of the pocket chart and cards with words such as *balls, chairs,* and *desks* on the other side. After giving the class time to talk to a partner, Lorena asked whether anyone could determine what she was thinking when she sorted the words. Students shared that "es" was added to one set of cards and "s" was added to the other. With Lorena's guidance, the class went on to discover words that the added "es" ended with "s," "ch," "sh," or "x." A new classroom chart was started following this activity, with word examples being added from children's independent reading and writing.

Learners in transition not only need to be tuned into the visual aspects of inflectional endings but also need to realize that the way words sound will change as well. When reading, children often struggle to correctly pronounce words that end with "ed," and misrepresent these words in writing. Having children collect words as they read and then sort them by how they sound can increase awareness of how the ending may change the sound of the entire word. They quickly realize that "ed" at the end of a word may sound like /d/, /ed/, or /t/. As they read, they write any words they find with an "ed" ending on a piece of paper, so they are the ones collecting the words for study. These words are then used for whole-group, small-group, and individual activities. Because the words are collected from texts being read in class, they provide practice at an appropriate level and ensure that students recognize the link between reading, writing, and word study.

High-Frequency Words

Readers in transition have already developed a core of known words and will need to continue learning more. As the texts they read and write become more complex, they encounter a broader range of vocabulary. It is increasingly important for students to quickly recognize parts they know and effectively engage in strategic action to solve new words so they can maintain the momentum necessary to read with meaning and comprehension.

Teaching children systems for learning new words is an important part of moving them toward independence. Because their core of known words continues to grow quickly, they cannot depend on the teacher to guide them in learning each new word. One teacher helped students become aware of how to learn new words as a part of their word work together. The chart in Figure 3.4, developed with students during direct instruction, taught them a system for learning words.

As children move from primary to intermediate grades, the high-frequency words they encounter generally become more complex. When introducing new words to children, it is helpful to teach them to look closely at the word, noticing parts that may be easy and/or difficult. This seems like a simple task, but, in doing so, we are asking students to look closely and notice small and sometimes confusing visual features of words. This is important, since reading high-frequency words requires visual memory. We ask students to look carefully at each word, say it, and then try writing the word quickly while not looking. To help them learn to check on themselves, we ask them to look at how they wrote the word before checking the spelling, to see whether the word "looks right." Building this routine helps children learn to monitor their spelling not only on tests but also when writing.

Figure 3.4   Chart for Learning Words

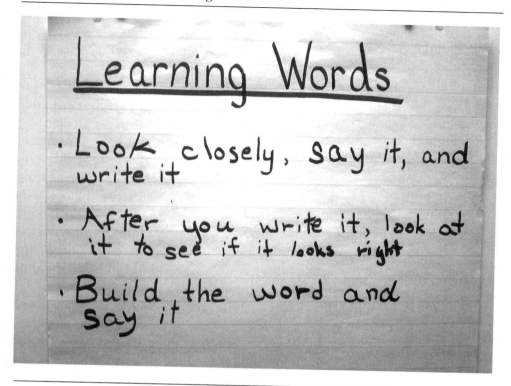

Learning Words

• Look closely, say it, and write it

• After you write it, look at it to see if it looks right

• Build the word and say it

Another activity regularly used to help children learn high-frequency words is building the words using letter tiles or magnetic letters. Manipulating the letters to form words makes children think not only about letters needed for a particular word but also about how to order the letters. Students can also form a word, mix it up, and put the letters back into correct order (Cunningham, 1999). Repeatedly doing this alone and in small groups will help sharpen their ability to know when the word "looks right," the visual processing necessary for both reading and writing.

Vocabulary

Children also need knowledge of word meanings. Vocabulary development is critical for reading comprehension and learning (Nagy, 2003). Developing an extensive listening, speaking, reading, and writing vocabulary is necessary in any instructional program (NICHHD, 2001). The larger the reader's vocabulary, the easier it is to make sense of text. Vocabulary learning in the early grades typically takes place through engagement in conversation, being read to by adults, and children's own reading (Armbruster et al., 2001). As the texts children read become more complex, there are more opportunities for vocabulary development to happen through independent reading. While we expect children to read at home, many children in our classes do all their independent reading in school. It is up to us to provide extensive time for independent reading. Studies show that children who read a lot learn about 8 words per day—more than 3,000 words per year—while those who don't do so learn about 2 words per day—about 700 words per year (Ohanian, 2002). Providing opportunities to read and motivating children to read are essential.

In the transition years, intentional teaching of vocabulary during language arts is necessary for increasing what children learn on their own through independent reading. Direct instruction should focus on learning specific words as well as teaching children to determine word meaning from word structures, like prefixes and suffixes. Children also need to learn how to determine word meaning by using the context while reading on their own. In the primary grades, teachers often discuss new words during and after read alouds as a way to build vocabulary (Beck, McKeown, & Kucan, 2002). As children move into the transition years, learning strategies to determine word meanings while reading text independent of the teacher is an important instructional focus, since children cannot be introduced to every word they may encounter.

Teachers must be deliberate in encouraging children to notice words and be excited about using new words in their oral and written language. Beck and colleagues (2002) suggest teachers routinely select two or three words to introduce from a read aloud to extend the vocabulary of students in the class. The words chosen should be ones used by more mature language users and be more precise vocabulary for a concept already understood by the students. For example, one teacher selected the word *infant*. She knew the concept of *baby* was understood by the class and believed *infant* to be a word with generative possibilities to other words such as *newborn* and *toddler*, as well as *infancy*. It would also be a word students could use in science as they studied life cycles of animals.

Another teacher kept a chart of "interesting words" that grew from read alouds. She selected two or three words from the read-aloud story to discuss and reinforce with children. She did this by using the words as much as possible in oral exchanges with students as many times as possible throughout the day. Other times, children noticed words and asked to put them on the chart. For example, a child heard the word *heave* in a story. He raised his hand and said that he didn't understand, since no one in the story had "thrown up." In this story, the character "heaved a ball." The teacher talked about the meaning of *heaved* as "to throw," and a girl in the group asked to add it to the class chart. After the story was finished, *heave* went up on the chart, and they again discussed its meaning. Children in this class were so excited about words, they filled many charts with interesting words and used them in their speech and writing. They had had a lot of exposure to the words because the teacher found ways to use them and she encouraged the children to try them. There were so many chances to see, hear, and use the words that the students were readily able to recognize and understand them in their reading.

Teaching children to use contextual information to determine word meaning is critical. Many texts children read provide parenthetical information about word meaning, but children don't always understand how to use it. Textual information can also be used to infer meaning from how a word is used, and children may need to read beyond the unknown word to determine meaning. One way to share the task and assist children in effectively using context is to have an overhead projector, with copies of pages from various books used to think aloud and model ways to figure out word meanings. Using big books is another successful approach for this instruction. To allow for follow-up practice, children can use a word journal during reading to record unknown words they encounter. Once the word is listed, they use the context and what they know about words to make a prediction of meaning (Cappellini, 2006). Figure 3.5 shows an example. In this example, one teacher was able to use the context while reading *Dr. DeSoto* (Steig, 1982) to read past the word *hoisted* and use the phrase "hoisted up to the patient's mouth" to predict a meaning for the word.

Figure 3.5   Word Journal

New words or phrases	What I know about the words	What I think the words mean
Book: Dr. DeSoto		
hoisted up to the patient's mouth	had to get up high with help	lifted up
caressed the new tooth with his tongue	rubbed his tongue over his tooth	rubbed it softly

The entries in the word journal may be discussed in a guided-reading group, with the whole class, or in a literature circle. The teacher can talk about words with the children and discuss their predictions and the actual meanings of the words. This activity not only helps children attend to words while they are reading, it guides their thinking with minimal support from the teacher. Following these supported activities, we can then observe how children determine meaning when reading independently.

Despite the heavy focus on phonics and high-frequency words in most word study programs, deliberate attention to vocabulary development is an important part of literacy instruction. Readers and writers in transition attempt to use more precise language in their writing and encounter more specific vocabulary in texts they read. Content language in science and social studies also becomes more challenging. Through lessons that address vocabulary development, teachers are able to provide necessary support for students as they begin to take on these additional challenges.

Word Walls and Charts

Word walls have been used in elementary classrooms for a number of years in a variety of ways. We continue to reflect on the purpose of word walls and have refined our use of them. For them to be useful in helping students build understanding of words and how they work, we want to make use of several different types of word walls. The focus in the transitional grades goes beyond creating collections of high-frequency words and simple word family charts often seen in primary classrooms. More attention is paid to structural features of words, more complex phonics patterns, and increasingly specific vocabulary. As children move into intermediate grades, word walls reflect this shift to structural analysis and also contain sections for Latin and Greek roots, affixes, or words with ties to other languages.

A visitor surveying the walls in Ruth's classroom would notice an easily recognizable word wall on a magnetic chalkboard near the large-group gathering area. Words are written on white cards with magnetic strips glued to the back, and they are organized in lists under each letter of the alphabet. The words on this word wall are all high-frequency words from a list Ruth's district has developed for second grade. During each grading period, students are expected to master 30 new words. Ruth pretests students on the words and chooses to first focus her instruction on words missed by most of the students.

When adding words to this word wall, Ruth takes time to introduce students to the words, help them learn ways to notice things about the words, and discuss how they might learn new words. Taking time to teach and scaffold children in this way, by drawing their attention to important visual features of words, moves them toward independence in knowing how to learn new words on their own.

Often, children are confused by words that sound or look similar, and to address this confusion, one of the children in Ruth's class suggested they make a sign warning others about these types of words. Soon, a poster with the heading "Tricky Alert" appeared near the word wall. Listed underneath were the words *went, want,* and *what.* Later, the children added meanings for the three words to help themselves remember which was which. Other charts were created to help children sort words they felt were difficult, such as *are,* which sounds like the letter "r" but certainly looks different. Ruth took this as a sign her students were internalizing the ability to think about words and ways to learn them.

High-frequency words are placed on the word wall only a few at a time. As children demonstrate the ability to read and write a word quickly and correctly, the words are retired by removing them from the wall. In our experience, word walls that contain too many words at one time are overwhelming to many children. It becomes difficult to quickly locate a needed word, and often words are left on the word wall that all or most of the children in the class already know. Removing known words is one way to keep the number of words meaningful and manageable. The following conversation took place one day as the class prepared to remove words from the wall:

Ruth: I've noticed lately that the word "said" has become an easy word for most of you. When you come to it in your reading, you read it quickly, and when you are writing, you are able to write it without having to stop and check.

Jacob: Yeah, it's like it's stuck in our brains.

Yesenia: We don't really need it on there [the word wall] anymore.

Ruth: That's right! This word wall is where we keep the words that we are trying to learn. When we've learned how to read and write them quickly, we keep them in our brains. So, what do you think? Can we take this one off the word wall, and keep it in our heads?

Children: Yes!

Reflecting on words learned and why they are removed from the word wall is important in helping children understand that the words on the word wall should be words we want to become "automatic"—words that can be read and written with accuracy and fluency. This moves the role of the word wall beyond a classroom resource to a holding place for words the children are working to make part of their known core of high-frequency words.

On other walls around Ruth's room, visitors would see many charts containing word collections that fit phonics patterns studied by the class. These smaller word walls serve a different purpose than the one containing high-frequency words. As students learn about various sound-to-letter relationships, charts are created by the class to collect examples that fit the pattern. When studying blends, for example, Ruth and her students created charts containing blends at the beginning of words, such as *pl*ay and *sw*im. Later, the children refined this collection, listing words with "s" blends (such as *sl*ip, *st*op, and *sm*all) or words with blends containing "r" (such as *pr*actice, *br*eak, and *tr*ap). As their study of blends continued, children started noticing that some words contained blends at the end (such as p*art* or e*nd*), and soon a new chart was created to hold examples of this type of word.

Ruth's classroom also contains posters created by the students to illustrate multiple-meaning words, depicting a sentence and a picture for each of the meanings for a word. In other small spaces throughout the room, posters feature words with common abbreviations. Other charts collect words that fit into various categories based on word meaning or words that represent common grammar concepts, such as nouns and verbs, contractions, or antonyms and synonyms.

Word charts may also be used to help with vocabulary development and content-area knowledge. Word walls for science and social studies may contain words for weather or words used to identify parts of a community and are on charts that may include diagrams and maps to categorize the terms. Word walls have also been used to focus on holiday words or interesting words students encounter in their reading. We want to encourage students to notice words they feel are special or find interesting. These words are carefully displayed in the room, and children can often be observed using their "special words" in conversation and in their independent writing.

Having word walls and charts that serve different purposes helps children organize their learning and more effectively use these classroom resources. Because students play an active role in creating the charts, they take ownership of them and use them to support their learning. Drawing attention to word patterns while collecting examples helps children internalize word study concepts. Having charts available for children as they write provides a reference for independent problem solving. Evidence that children use these charts can be seen when they turn to refer to a chart while thinking about how to record something in their writing. In reading, children recognize visual patterns they have studied and use them to help quickly decode new words. One day, Teresa, a third-grade teacher, was working with a small group of children at the guided-reading table. As they read the text, Jaime came to the word *chest,* which was not a known word for him. He paused, then turned and looked at a chart on the wall containing words with "st" at the end. After looking back to the text, he correctly read the word "chest." He then looked up at Teresa, exclaiming, "Hey! The 'st' in chest is just like the words with 'st' on our chart!"

LINKING TO THE REAL WORK OF READING AND WRITING

A typical concern of teachers is that students don't seem to apply their knowledge from word study when they are engaged in the reading and writing of text. This caused us to examine our own instruction of linking these areas of literacy learning. We realized we needed to make the connections more obvious for students by providing explicit instruction and modeling ways to use what they have been taught, as readers and writers, through our language during instruction. Through continual discussion and shared activities, we help students see connections and understand how to transfer their learning from one situation to another. Peter Johnston (2004) states, "It seems the less compartmentalized we make children's learning lives, the more likely they are to transfer their strategic problem-solving to other situations" (p. 44). The goal is for children to become flexible, applying strategies to solve problems (Johnston, 2004). Integrating literacy instruction as well as content instruction enables students to connect their learning and to use what they know in a variety of contexts. This type of linking can and should continue over time, with the clear expectation that what is learned and practiced during word study is to be applied when reading and writing in all parts of the curriculum.

REFLECTION

As the sophistication of what students are learning in word study increases, the ability of learners in transition to apply word patterns, strategies, and concepts should become more flexible, fluent, and accurate. The shift to more complex understanding of how to represent sounds with various letter patterns, the ability to think flexibly and efficiently about words, and the refining of specific vocabulary indicate that students are prepared for the challenges that await them in the intermediate grades.

4

Reading

One fall day, Julie, a second-grade teacher, was working with a guided-reading group, when a girl approached the table and tried to get her attention. Wanting the student to remember that she was not to interrupt the group, Julie waved her away. A few minutes later, the girl reappeared, this time shoving a book in front of Julie and blurting out, "But this is really important—an emergency! Did you know that this is a *real* book, and I can read it all myself?" Up to this point, almost everything this student had read had been chosen and introduced to her by a teacher or was a book she had heard read aloud. For most transitional readers, the realization that they can choose and read many books on their own is pivotal in their lives as readers. As children reach this point, their needs as readers grow beyond gaining control over early reading behaviors and basic comprehension, and the focus of reading instruction shifts toward developing independence in processing a wider variety of texts at more complex levels of comprehension as students take more responsibility for their own learning.

At the beginning of Chapter 1, we observed the differences between reading workshop in first and third grades. Immediately apparent were the changes in the workshop format and the abilities of the children to process and respond to text independently. In our work with a wide range of teachers and students in a variety of classrooms, we recognized significant threads in this transition process. We have categorized these threads as increasing independence and stamina, strengthening the depth of comprehension, and shifting from oral responses to written responses. As learners progress, we must adjust the content and format of our instruction to meet the needs of students. In this chapter, we explore the changing needs of transitional readers and what instruction is appropriate after children gain control over early reading behaviors. While we recognize that readers in transition are encountering many diverse challenges as they read more difficult and widely varied texts, our focus will remain on the key areas we have defined as critical during this stage of learning (see Figure 4.1).

Figure 4.1   Change Over Time in Reading Development

	Early Elementary	*Transition*	*Intermediate*
Reading	• Develops basic print concepts • Begins to control early reading strategies and behaviors • Begins to monitor own reading • Self-corrects occasionally • Relies on picture support • Uses limited experience with various genres • Builds a small core of high-frequency words • Reads aloud most of the time • Comprehends basic story line for independently read text • Responds to texts verbally • Demonstrates more complex understanding of texts read aloud • Illustrates as a way to respond to text reading	• Develops and uses a large core of high-frequency words • Strengthens control over early reading behaviors and strategies • Maintains reading for longer periods of time • Develops more complex understanding of texts read independently • Responds to texts both verbally and in writing • Reads silently most of the time • Consistently monitors own reading • Problem solves using a variety of sources of information • Can read a wide variety of genres • Reads more fluently in meaningful phrases, with some attention to punctuation • Writes simple responses to texts independently	• Recognizes and accurately uses a large core of known words • Navigates texts subconsciously • Maintains deep understanding of text • Reads for extended periods of time and reads texts over several days • Responds to text both verbally and in writing • Monitors reading, able to efficiently and flexibly problem solve without losing momentum or meaning • Is familiar with a wide variety of genres • Reads expressively in meaningful phrases with natural-sounding fluency

GETTING TO KNOW A READER IN TRANSITION

In addition to the chart (Figure 4.1) that outlines changes in reading during the transition years, looking closely at one reader helps us become even more aware of the abilities of transitional readers. We start by considering what Brianna has under control when processing and responding to text and what she is beginning to try. We use this information to shift both the format and content of our instruction to meet her needs.

Brianna entered second grade as an early transitional reader. She liked to read and had many early reading behaviors well under control. Her core of high-frequency words was growing rapidly, and she easily used those words to help move through text and monitor herself as she read. Brianna was usually able to process text at a surface level without requiring much assistance. While she noticed and occasionally used pictures to support her reading, Brianna was shifting more of her attention to the words as her means for making sense of the text. The stories she read contained simple plots with characters who acted in predictable ways, and she was able to demonstrate basic comprehension of what she read. Brianna had different strategies to use when she encountered difficulty and was working to coordinate the use of those strategies to problem solve and monitor her reading. As is typical of many students early in the transitional stage of reading, Brianna sometimes struggled when presented with a new genre or unfamiliar text formats. Brianna spent time each day reading independently and was able to stay engaged with books for 10 to 15 minutes at a time. Brianna used this time not only for processing whole texts but also for leafing through new books and focusing on the pictures to gather information about what happened in the stories. She frequently chose and attempted to read books her teacher had read aloud many times, making them familiar and easy to retell. Brianna rarely attempted to read a new book during independent-reading time, although she would often attempt reading parts of a new story.

Readers like Brianna, who are just moving into the transitional stage of reading, need to develop more complex comprehension strategies as well as the stamina and flexibility to be successful in the intermediate grades. Explicit instruction in comprehension strategies is needed, and as the reader encounters more complex plots and characters and a wider range of genres, there will be many opportunities for practice. By making use of instructional contexts that vary in level of teacher support, we can provide opportunities tailored to the needs of readers as they move through a transition process. As we meet the needs of children entering this transition while at the same time considering the skills and strategies required for work in the intermediate grades, we need to shift instruction.

With an understanding of the profile of a reader entering the transitional phase of literacy, it is important to look ahead at literacy abilities children need for success in the intermediate grades. Holding these as goals for reading instruction, we can look ahead to what a reader might look like in the later stages of transition and early stages of competence (Alexander, 2005/2006). Competent intermediate children read with fluency and automaticity, placing little conscious attention on the basic skills and strategies of text reading. They are successful at surface-level comprehension, such as retelling, providing the facts, making predictions, and understanding basic plot structures. They are able and willing to read a range and variety of genres, including both fiction and nonfiction materials. They understand how to confront the various types of problems that arise in text reading and have effective, efficient ways to successfully solve those problems independently. Their focus is in connecting with text more deeply through the content and author's purpose, making connections across texts and critiquing and analyzing for many purposes. Readers in the intermediate grades routinely respond in writing to texts they have read, and their responses reflect more complex comprehension. They are self-motivated to read and will support their own specific goals and interests, reducing the need for teacher direction, motivation, and monitoring (Alexander, 2005/2006).

For children to become more independent as readers, we must work to increase their abilities to take personal responsibility for learning and to work independently. It is up to us to organize our instructional contexts to facilitate that growth. Changing how children work independently during reading time can assist in moving children to independence as well as help them sustain reading work over time.

DEVELOPING STAMINA

One of the biggest jobs for transitional readers is to build stamina. When we talk about *stamina,* we mean that the reader must not only be able to read longer text or read for longer periods of time but must also do so while maintaining comprehension. As children encounter books with complex plots and ideas, more events, and more highly developed characters, they become cognitively tired. Simply increasing the time spent reading independently is not enough to develop the type of broad staying power readers in transition need. Along with a gradual increase in reading time, we found that students needed direct instruction in how to maintain comprehension as they read. This is more challenging than we realize, and it takes time to develop.

Readers in transition need to gradually increase the amount of time they spend independently processing text successfully, and teachers need to become careful observers of students in order to support this shift. We begin by knowing our readers and watching carefully as they read, while at the same time being sensitive to the signs that they've reached their limit. Often, children will become disengaged with the task of reading, and we notice them turning pages aimlessly as they seem to lose track of what is happening in a story. Early in the process, readers in transition tire much more quickly and easily than more experienced readers. Longer, more complex plots require more stamina in both basic reading strategies as well as comprehension.

CHANGES IN WORKSTATIONS

In addition to changes in time and focus as readers, children grow to need different independent activities. As they begin to transition as readers, they may be in classrooms where they have been moving through three to four literacy workstations during reading workshop. Literacy workstations are areas in the room set aside for children to work independently or with others to reinforce and extend their learning (Diller, 2003). Work in these stations provides opportunities for children to explore literacy concepts they have learned through direct instruction and previous guided practice.

As they move into the intermediate grades, they will spend more time reading and responding to text, leaving literacy stations behind. To set the stage for this shift, teachers can organize their literacy stations so the change seems natural. Having all students begin with independent reading helps children develop the habit of moving from a minilesson directly to their own reading. In Marc's second-grade classroom, all children start the workshop reading independently for about 15 minutes. At the end of that time, they move into workstations. Students typically spend time at two different stations and engage in activities such as picture sorts, writing short stories or notes, reading with a partner, or listening to stories on tape. As the time spent doing independent reading gradually increases, time for working in stations decreases until students reach the point where they have time for only one station each day. Putting independent reading first ensures that this will be a more natural progression, without the need for abrupt change.

Though they may not have station work in the intermediate grades, there is great value in having transitional readers work at tasks designed to meet their needs as readers, writers, and word solvers during the reading time. As they move through the year, these tasks become more complex and require more time to complete. While tasks early in the year focus on early reading, writing, and word-solving strategies, the tasks become more complex as the year progresses. At the word study station, for example, students may spend time sorting pictures by beginning, middle, or ending sounds. By midyear, children are capable of attending to larger chunks of words and have moved to sorting words by larger visual features and patterns. They may also be generating new words using patterns studied during word study. While working at the writing station early in the year, learners may have been writing simple two- and three-sentence stories. Now, they have the skills to carry a project over several days, writing more complex stories and experimenting with other genres. Some children may even take out writing workshop folders and continue working on pieces started during writing workshop.

In Marc's classroom, the following conversation resulted in decreasing the number of stations children moved through each day:

Marc: During our workshop today, several of you asked if you could keep working at your first station instead of going on to the next one. Do you think we need to make a change?

Alexis: Yeah. I keep wanting to finish what I'm doing, but when it's time to change, I'm not done yet.

Bradley: And I wasn't done with my chapter. . . . Can I just keep reading?

Marc: Well, it seems like you are doing work that takes longer now, and it makes sense to keep reading if you are not at a good place to stop. Maybe if you did just one station each day, it would be better.

August: I think so. Then I don't have to think about whether or not I have time to do what I want to do at that station. I could just do it and think about that.

When transitional readers find they cannot get to all the stations because they are reading independently for longer periods of time or because the tasks they are completing are more complex, this indicates the students are ready to eliminate one or more of the stations.

GRADUALLY DECREASING SMALL-GROUP GUIDED READING

We know that successful intermediate readers do not need high teacher support to process every text they encounter. While still receiving direct instruction in comprehending strategies and more complex word analysis, they are capable of choosing and reading books on their own, with the teacher checking often to monitor progress and provide support. Many readers in transition, while still relying on teacher support for much of what they read, are beginning to encounter more texts they can read without support. In the classroom setting, children who are beginning to read more successfully on their own may not need daily groups with the teacher in order to continue making progress. Teachers should carefully consider which guided-reading groups might meet fewer times per week and which groups still require daily interaction with the teacher and guided lessons.

If daily guided-reading groups are a large part of the reading routine, being left to the task of reading without immediate support and feedback might seem frightening to some students. Teachers should be prepared to hear cries of, "Why didn't you call my group? When is it our turn?" If we are truly teaching for independence, our job is to make ourselves unnecessary. Not only is this difficult for students, it can also be hard for us as teachers to realize that some students really don't need us. This process of gradually releasing responsibility for aspects of learning must take place as children transition from the primary to intermediate grades.

USING READING MINILESSONS

As readers spend more time reading independently and less time meeting with the teacher for guided reading, it becomes necessary to provide instruction in a context that allows children to use what they are learning while reading on their own. This means beginning a broadly defined reading workshop (Fountas & Pinnell, 2001) that includes a whole-group lesson to begin the workshop and options for small-group guided reading, literature circles, independent reading, and other independent literacy activities. Starting each workshop with a minilesson provides explicit instruction for students to apply during independent reading. When beginning to move into a reading workshop approach, minilessons are largely procedural and include learning how to use the classroom library, choosing a place to read independently, and the organization for sharing time at the end of the workshop. Teachers and children may chart the expectations for reading workshop and post them in a prominent place in the room. Figure 4.2 is an example of the chart Carla developed from procedural minilessons with her second-grade class. As the class was transitioning to a reading workshop, they had several lessons on what to do in reading workshop and used interactive writing to collaboratively develop this chart over several days.

Figure 4.2   Expectations for Reading Workshop

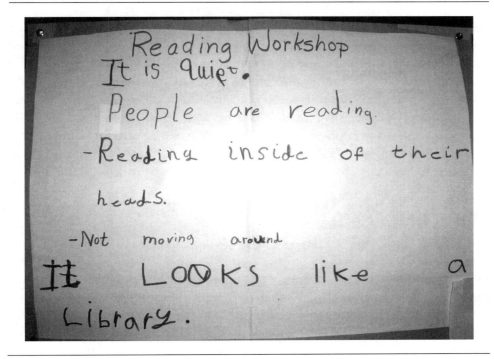

As the children settle into reading workshop, minilessons begin to shift toward preparing children to become more effective readers. Reading a book aloud as part of the minilesson can serve as a model for fluency and comprehension. This read-aloud process provides needed support to readers moving into the transitional stage, so they can be engaged in thinking about texts that may be above their individual reading levels. They need to "see and hear it" in action to get a feel for what they should begin to try on their own. When modeling a particular strategy, we begin with some direct instruction. For example, the teacher may say, "Readers use the author's words to help them make a picture in their heads of what is happening in the story." She reads a story to her students, pausing to point out words that helped her create a mental image or that caused her mental image to change. Over time, this teacher would continue to model use of the strategy, inviting students to join. We need to be careful not to "kill books" by turning every read aloud into an important lesson, but we should not underestimate the power of using this time for reading instruction. After modeling a strategy or behavior, the teacher may ask the children to join in by responding during the read aloud.

Teachers might also consider using shared-reading experiences as part of their minilessons. In shared reading, teacher and students read together from an enlarged text that all can see or from individual copies of the same text. Practicing skills and strategies together in a text that all can see provides a highly supportive context for learning and pushes the children to be as active as the teacher. The shared-reading experience is often overlooked by teachers with transitional readers, particularly as instruction moves beyond early reading strategies. For example, using shared reading to help children locate places in text where an inference is made can help children better comprehend the text when reading. While reading the poem "The Secret" (Anonymous, 2003), Vanessa guided her students to use words in the text to figure out the secret, even though the author never tells. Her students inferred that the "secret" was a bird's nest with eggs. When asked what words helped them, they pointed out the phrases "because he built the—I shan't tell the rest" and "laid the four little—somethings—in it" (p. 230) as clues that supported their inference. Using shared reading during this minilesson allowed all of Vanessa's students to learn how to make and support inferences in a highly supportive and successful context.

TEACHING CHILDREN HOW TO CHOOSE BOOKS

Lessons about how to choose books are not only appropriate but also necessary for transitional readers as they become more independent. They have learned a great deal about how books work and know their own abilities to take on this task for themselves. Children are expected to become experienced in choosing "just right" books for themselves (Routman, 2002). Talking together about what makes a book "easy" or "hard" can help readers move toward thinking about what makes a book "just right." When considering what makes a book easy, children often mention that they know all the words or the book doesn't have many words. They may notice the pictures are helpful. Books children have read or heard many times may also fall into this category. Teachers can help children realize that being able to read a book fluently may also indicate it is an easy book. But above all, if we want students to view reading as more than word calling, we must include being able to understand and talk about what was read in order to ultimately determine how easy or challenging a text is for a reader.

Thinking about what makes a book challenging is also a fairly easy task for most transitional readers. They immediately think about books with a lot of words and few pictures. Books containing words or ideas the readers don't understand also fit in this category. Children who have had minilessons about making connections may say that if they cannot somehow connect to the book, it may be a difficult text to read. Teachers should also help readers understand that even if they can pronounce all the words but don't know what the story is about, the text is too challenging.

Just-right books fit somewhere in between. Readers may need to slow down and think through ideas or solve words, but most of the text is accessible and comprehendible for the reader. Readers of just-right books can understand and tell what the story is about. Figure 4.3 shows a chart created by the students in Marc's room, describing how they could tell whether a book was easy, difficult, or just right.

Figure 4.3   Choosing Books

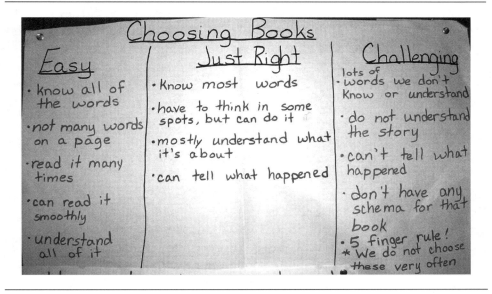

Teachers must take into consideration that interest and familiarity can affect how easy or difficult a text may be for a reader. Children obsessed with dinosaurs frequently choose to read books that would be much too difficult if it weren't for their focused interest in that topic. Likewise, familiar characters or authors may also help children read text that would otherwise be beyond their reach. Transitional readers often choose to read series books, where the predictability of the characters offers a sense of comfort and support.

It is not enough to instruct transitional readers on how to choose books. We must also make sure they independently practice making their own book choices and have time to reflect on the outcome of their choices. At the end of each reading time, we find it helpful to gather to discuss the day's reading work. This is a time when children can bring independent-reading books they chose in order to share why they thought a particular book would be just right and how it went when they actually sat down to read it. With the teacher there to guide their reflection, this type of sharing shifts students back to a more supportive context that confirms learning and helps clear misconceptions. Learning to make appropriate book choices is initially challenging for transitional readers, and they require ample opportunity to practice and receive feedback.

LITERATURE CIRCLES

Another way in which teachers can help develop independence in transitional readers is to provide opportunities for participation in literature circles. Literature circles consist of small groups of children who agree to read the same text or similar text with a common theme or author. After reading the entire text or an agreed-upon section of the text, the children meet to discuss what they have read and their reactions to the reading. As children become more comfortable with discussions during highly interactive read alouds and demonstrate the ability to take an active role in conversations about books, they are ready to participate in student-led literature circles. While some teachers advocate beginning literature circles in the primary grades, we believe it is more effective to gradually guide children into independent literature circles. While students will undoubtedly learn from their reading and participation in the discussions, much of their energy at first will be focused on knowing how to act in a literature circle. Teachers establish ground rules such as "Everybody talks, everybody listens" to ensure that the groups stay focused on the task of discussing books. We found guided reading to be a good place to teach and practice behaviors children will need when participating in literature circles. Initially, students will need the teacher to facilitate the negotiation of when and where the group will meet and how much of the text must be read prior to the meeting.

Transitional readers also need guidance with the content of discussions. Early literature circles are much more successful if the participants agree to discuss what they learned about a certain character or what questions they had as they read. Students should be prepared to show evidence in the text that supports what they say in group. One popular method for preparation is to have children mark places in the text with sticky notes to help them be prepared for discussion. Other teachers meet briefly with the children to chart reminders to help them stay focused. Figure 4.4 shows a chart one third-grade teacher and a group of students created to help guide the discussion of the group after reading *The Stories Julian Tells*, by Ann Cameron (1989). Focusing on a particular aspect of the text helped the children get their conversation started and kept it centered on the text. The chart also guided them to pay attention to how the author developed and revealed the characters in the story. Though they met with the teacher to create the chart, the students were able to successfully meet on their own to discuss the book.

While literature circles are mostly student led, the teacher may sit nearby and listen in as the groups meet. This allows the teacher to identify areas in which the students need further instruction or more support. Some teachers also have children write a simple reflection after meeting with the group. These reflections may be structured as a means for providing valuable feedback to the teacher. One child, writing a reflection

Figure 4.4   *The Stories Julian Tells* Chart

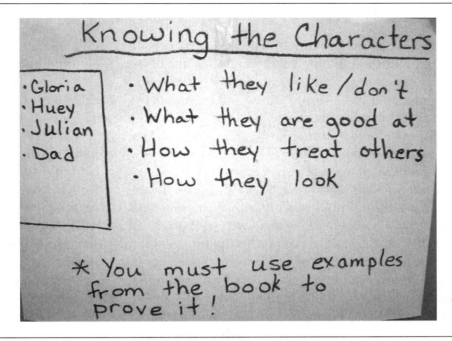

about her experience in a literature circle, stated, "I thought I knew about this book until I talked to the other kids in the group!"

STRENGTHENING COMPREHENSION

While increasing independence and stamina are certainly important for transitional readers, we must keep in mind that our ultimate goal is for children to comprehend what they read. As we think about deeper comprehension and transitional readers, we certainly consider things such as using schema, making mental images, and inferring (Keene & Zimmerman, 1997; Miller, 2002). Although comprehending strategies are important and are the focus of much of the instruction across the reading work time, we found that readers in transition also met other challenges when it came to comprehending. As they encountered more complex plots and characters in stories they read, students struggled to know what information was important and how and why characters changed in response to events in the story. We found it necessary to provide high support as they encountered text that could not be finished in one sitting. In addition, following dialogue and understanding which character was talking became more difficult. Children were accustomed to reading text in which dialogue was followed by the word *said* and the name of a character. They were now reading stories with unassigned dialogue. Pages were filled with conversation between two or more characters. Both shared and guided reading provided highly supported contexts for direct instruction on how to follow dialogue, and our conferences with individuals during independent-reading time enabled us to make sure that students were maintaining comprehension as they read.

Chapter books provide transitional readers with other challenges. Not only must they determine what is important to remember, they must be able to remember what they read from one day to the next. Being able to carry meaning over several days and come back to a text ready to read is a new experience for young readers. Teachers often read chapter books aloud to students and help guide them in summarizing previous events, understandings, and questions before reading a new chapter. This can help them prepare to face the same challenge on their own.

The structure of chapter books provides opportunities for readers to learn how these books are organized. In some books, each chapter is a separate story, such as *Frog and Toad Are Friends* (Lobel, 1970). Books like *Mr. Putter and Tabby Bake the Cake* (Rylant, 1994) are one story, with each chapter presenting a new episode of the story. A study of how chapter books are organized can also help transitional readers learn how to organize their thinking while reading longer texts. One teacher noticed that many readers just beginning to read chapter books believed they needed to read the whole text at once and others stopped at any point in the story instead of looking for natural breaks in the text. We need to teach and model stopping points so children can do this in a more meaningful way when they are reading independently.

Learning how to preview books can help readers set themselves up to better comprehend what they read. This may be an unfamiliar strategy for some transitional readers, and they often need direct instruction in how to do it. Before reading aloud to students, teachers can guide them to look at the title and cover of the book, thinking and talking together to predict what might happen in the story. Not only does this help support understanding, it sets the stage for the children to begin learning how to introduce books to themselves as well as enabling them to start thinking about the meaning of the text before reading. If we expect children to self-select books and read independently during reading workshop time, they must be able to predict and set a mental stage for the reading that is to come. Inviting children to share this task during shared and guided reading provides valuable practice in a supportive setting before expecting them to take on the task for themselves. Figure 4.5 is a chart created by Tanisha's second-grade class to remind them what to do before they read.

In addition to learning strategies for understanding what they read, transitional readers must also learn to monitor their comprehension and recognize when they don't understand and know what to do to handle this problem independently. One day, Lori, a third-grade teacher, was conferring with Ana during independent-reading time:

Lori: I see that you are reading *The Magic Tree House: The Knight Before Dawn* [Osborne, 1993]: How is it going?

Ana: Not good. I don't think I understand it.

Lori: How do you know?

Figure 4.5   Before Reading

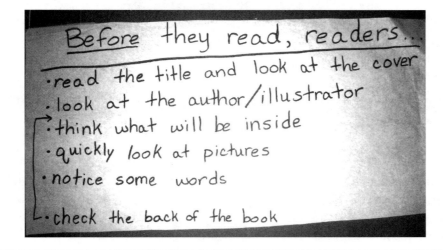

Ana: Well, on the chart, we said that if we don't remember what happened, it means we don't understand (see Figure 4.6).

Lori: It is important to understand what we read, and you noticed that you didn't understand. So what do you think you might try?

Ana: I think I'm going to read it slow so I can think more . . . and also read another one of these [*Magic Tree House*] books so I can make some connections.

Lori: Okay. How about I check back with you soon to see if that works?

Figure 4.6   Monitoring Comprehension

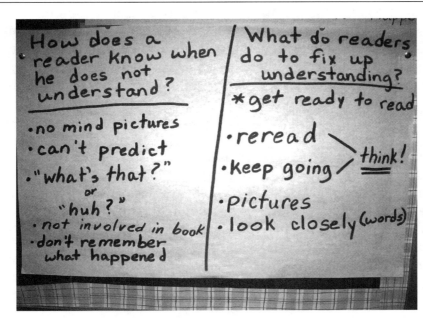

In this example, Lori was able to recognize Ana's ability to know when she wasn't comprehending and also support her attempts to use a resource created during a minilesson to solve the problem on her own. Checking back in allows Lori to monitor whether or not Ana needs more support with this critical piece of comprehension.

SHARED READING FOR COMPREHENSION AND FLUENCY

Shared-reading lessons for beginning readers focus on early reading behaviors, such as directionality, using the initial letter and the picture to figure out unknown words, and using known words to check their reading; however, shared reading also serves as a model for fluency and can include comprehension discussion. As readers move into the transitional stage of reading, most of them no longer need a highly supported activity for learning about early reading behaviors. In our experience, transitional readers benefit from shared reading as a highly supported practice in comprehension and fluency.

While teachers of early or emergent readers may point to each word while doing shared reading to support one-to-one matching and directionality, transitional readers do not need this type of support. In fact, pointing word by word often hampers their ability to read fluently. Teachers may choose to point to the beginning of each line of text or smoothly slide a pointer under the text. Children and teachers can practice reading fluently together during shared-reading lessons. Previewing the text for places where they may pause, stop, or read words with a particular expression helps students realize that punctuation and special text fonts indicate how their reading should sound. When hearing how a piece should sound and reading with a group, children receive valuable support in moving toward more natural-sounding fluency in their own reading.

Shared-reading time is also a valuable time to help children become more strategic readers. Transitional readers have some strategies under control for decoding and solving problems as they read. They have also begun to learn more comprehending strategies to use for enhancing their understanding. Reading a text together, followed by a discussion to engage in complex comprehension, provides an opportunity to return to the text to locate evidence supporting comments and points of view, something transitional readers initially struggle to do on their own.

Reading a text together and discussing the strategies that are most helpful for solving specific reading problems enable children to see and participate in strategic action. The whole-group experience fosters a sense of community learning and allows struggling readers to participate successfully with their peers. This type of teacher-supported activity is done during guided-reading lessons.

The children in Ellen's third-grade class had been working on what to do when they encountered words they could say but did not understand.

Many shared-reading experiences had focused on what to try when this happened. Ellen continually reminded the children that they could use these strategies when reading on their own as well as when reading with the whole class. One day, the children in one guided group encountered the word *contraption.* Not sure what the word meant, two of the children appealed to Ellen for help. She said, "Let's think about it." The children immediately looked back to the text to see whether there was a picture that could help. After quickly scanning the picture, they reread the sentence containing the word. "Oh, I know!" exclaimed one of the children, "It says he worked on his contraption for two days. This thing he's building is the contraption." The other child chimed in, "So, it's a thing you kind of invent." Without further prompting from Ellen, the children continued reading the text. The shared-reading lessons enabled these readers to practice something with high levels of support until they were able to take it on in more independent settings.

SHIFTING RESPONSES TO TEXT

Intermediate-grade readers will be expected to respond to text in writing, something with which primary readers are often unfamiliar. Since literacy learning is highly dependent on oral language, it makes sense to help children learn how to respond verbally to text before expecting them to be successful doing it in writing. Minilessons at the beginning of reading workshop, guided-reading lessons, and shared reading provide wonderful opportunities for teaching children strategies for thinking and talking about books.

Guided-reading groups provide great opportunities for children to practice conversations, as the groups are small and the topics clear. The challenge is to get them to take on more of the responsibility for conversations. In most primary and early transitional guided-reading groups, the conversation resembles the spokes of a wheel, with conversation flowing from each student to and from the teacher. The responsibility for redirecting comments to another child in the group or drawing others into the conversation rests with the teacher. The goal is for these conversations to begin to look more like spiderwebs, with talk bouncing back and forth between students, and the teacher being an equal participant, responsible for providing assistance only when needed.

A second-grade teacher concerned about the conversations in one of her guided-reading groups was struggling to get the students to talk to each other instead of only to her. Each time a student addressed her, she would gently ask the child to repeat the comment while looking at another member of the group. While this was successful in a limited way, she decided to take more drastic measures. As the group began to discuss the story they had read, she moved to sit at the edge of the group instead of the middle. This was a visual cue that the teacher was only one of several members in the group, and students gradually began to address one another. The teacher became the facilitator of conversation instead of the leader. Our goal is to have children doing most of the talking during guided-reading discussions, while we listen to learn how their thinking relates to their reading. We want to make sure we are not unintentionally limiting their thinking by controlling their conversations. As readers move into the late transitional stage, we continue to refine their ability to keep conversations going with less teacher support.

Early in the year, teachers begin talking with children about books, sometimes recording the thinking of the group on charts. Figure 4.7 shows a page from a class reading log. As they discussed what *schema* is and how it helps readers understand, the teacher and children in this example decided to write down what they noticed.

As readers move to the middle of the transitional stage, they are able to begin to write responses themselves. To ensure that students have the support they need to be successful, the task must be shared before we can expect children to take it on for themselves.

Figure 4.7   Page From Class Reading Log

Our ✳ schema helps make books easier to read. If we know about the stuff in a book, we understand better.

This happened with Brandon's Pokemon book, The 3 Little Pigs, and a book about seasons.

At this point, establishing a class reading log to model a written response to reading is helpful. The class reading log is written on a chart tablet and is used by the class to write their thoughts from whole-group readings. It is also used for learners to record what they are learning about being readers. After a read aloud or shared reading, the teacher models how to date the log entry, record the title, and write thoughts she had about the story. Asking children to contribute ideas enables them to see how their thinking will be represented in a reading-response log. Students may also be invited to add more of their thoughts to the entry during the reading work time. These added pieces can be discussed during the sharing time at the end of the workshop.

This task is not easy for transitional readers. They are still learning about ways readers organize their thinking while reading and about the kind of thinking that most helps with understanding. The added challenge of articulating those thoughts in writing should not be underestimated, and teachers need to take time to work with children on this task.

Alison was working with her students to think about a book she had just read aloud. As children were learning about mental images and discussing language in the story that helped them make pictures in their minds, they wrote several phrases in the class reading log. One child tentatively raised his hand: "Could we also write 'This is hard'?" Heads around the circle nodded. Clearly, he and his classmates still felt challenged by the task of writing responses to reading, even when practiced with peer and teacher support.

WRITING MORE DEVELOPED RESPONSES TO READING

After extended shared experiences and practice responding verbally to text, children late in the transitional stage are ready to write responses to reading independently. As they become more active in adding to the class reading log, they can shift to writing in individual reading logs. Initially, they will need to use classroom charts and the class reading log as models. Some children will write with clarity of thought and amaze and surprise us with their understanding. Others may be able only to tell what happened in their stories or explain why they liked a book. While our goal is certainly to have all our students write deeper responses, we recognize the importance of celebrating the progress of all children, wherever it is they begin their journeys. To take understandings and verbal responses and learn how to clearly express them in writing is a huge accomplishment.

SHARING TIME

As children begin to move through the transitional stage of reading, we monitor their progress in order to adjust our instruction to meet their needs. We want students to reflect on their learning. Building time at the end of each workshop session for reflection can help make the most of what children are learning as readers and managers of their own learning. We call this *sharing time*. During sharing time, we ask children questions, such as "What kind of worker were you today?" or "What did you do to help yourself become a better reader?" This helps them not only to become aware of their progress but also to learn to reflect on and identify what they need to learn next.

Readers in transition still need opportunities to refine the ability to be strategic, independent readers and learners. Continuing to share difficulties and successes at the end of each reading workshop provides children with a way to learn from each other by hearing the thinking and decisions others made when faced with difficulty. This sharing also enables teachers to pinpoint strategies or skills that may need to be introduced or retaught.

Sharing time provides transitional readers with an opportunity to reflect on themselves as readers and provides them with a chance to address what is challenging. With teacher guidance and support, the children can use this time to problem solve together or to ask for help with something on which they have been working. This is also a time for celebrations. Early in the year in one third-grade teacher's classroom, several children struggled with remembering they had an ongoing reading assignment. After several guided-reading sessions in which they had not read the assigned text, Trenton came up with a solution. He listed each chapter he was to read on a sticky note and placed the note on his nametag. Each day, at the start of independent-reading time, he checked the note to see where to begin reading. At the end of each session, he carefully crossed off the chapters he had finished. After determining this was successful, Trenton shared his strategy with the other children. The number of children "forgetting" to complete reading assignments dropped dramatically. Taking time to share a problem and celebrate Trenton's solution provided other students with a successful model for handling longer text over several days. Spending time with children and reflecting on the work done during workshop time and working together to solve problems that arise enables them to work with a higher degree of independence.

REFLECTION

As we reflect on the journey primary readers make and what lies ahead for them, we realize how important it is for us to continually adjust our instruction to meet their needs. By carefully considering their changing abilities, we keep them on the edge of their learning and guide them toward becoming independent readers who can demonstrate deeper understanding of text. By the end of this stage, children have shifted in their abilities as primary-grade readers and now more closely resemble readers in intermediate grades.

Knowing the kinds of adjustments to make in response to the capabilities and needs of transitional readers requires careful consideration and deliberate thought. Understanding when to make shifts is critical and calls on us to be sensitive observers of children. We know the students are ready for a shift when we notice certain things occurring during reading workshop. Children may act as follows:

- Want more time to complete tasks
- Have the ability to take on more complex work with less teacher support
- Carry single tasks over a number of days or break tasks into several steps
- Express thoughts in writing
- Express a preference for individual as opposed to shared response
- Remain engaged in independent reading for extended periods of time

This list is not all-inclusive. Teachers may note other behaviors indicating a need for change of format or content in reading instruction. We found one of the most important things to remember is that individuals and groups of students will move through this transitional stage at a different pace. Some children will continue to need a more supportive structure through second and well into third grade, while others are ready for more independence during second grade. In addition, children who are quite independent in one area may need much more teacher support in another. We consistently found that the most powerful skill for the teacher was to recognize the ongoing, changing capabilities and needs of transitional readers within reading workshop and to understand ways to thoughtfully adjust instruction in response to the specific strengths and needs of the children.

5

Writing

"I have writers who are all over the place. Some need a lot of support just getting words on the paper, and others are writing pages and pages," one teacher told us in frustration. Many teachers are asking how to meet the range of needs of writers in the transition years and move them to meet the writing standards for their grade levels. A few students in one second-grade class are an example of the range of writing abilities we see. Meredith entered second grade writing short, simple personal stories with words spelled accurately. She seemed to write safely with simple vocabulary, unwilling to take risks in writing words she didn't already know how to spell. In addition, she wrote slowly and took care forming each letter. Bryan was struggling as a writer. He seemed to have difficulty getting writing on the page. If the teacher sat with him and talked him through his thoughts, encouraging him and helping say words slowly as he wrote, then some writing made it to the page. On another part of the spectrum of second-grade writers, Korey wrote pages and pages of fantasy that were disjointed and read like stream of consciousness. His handwriting was hard to read, and many words, even simple words, were misspelled. He wrote hurriedly as ideas bounded out of his head. Still in the same class, Quinton was an accomplished second-grade writer. He thoughtfully planned his writing, using details and description. He stretched his writing into several genres, although for the most part he enjoyed learning and writing about different animals. He conscientiously worked to try out what he was learning through minilessons and individual conferences. Other students in the class completed the continuum of writing abilities typical in any second- or third-grade classroom.

In this chapter, we discuss the abilities and developmental issues of children in this age group and talk about how various writing contexts, such as interactive writing, shared writing, and writing workshop, can be used successfully in second and third grades. Included is a discussion using the analysis of children's writing to inform instructional decisions.

While there are variations in what children know and can do as writers, there are also many commonalities. As children begin to transition, their writing becomes more fluent and deliberate. Letter formation and handwriting are less of an issue, so children can write more volume in the same amount of time and for longer periods of time. As they move beyond the two to five simple sentences that characterize their writing in first grade, they begin to use more varied vocabulary and more complex language structures. Their use of accurately spelled high-frequency words increases, and they explore invented spellings for the less common words in their writing. They are using end punctuation correctly but are just beginning to revise and edit. They write longer pieces over several days by "adding on," an early form of revision. Although this longer writing may not flow well or hang together as a cohesive piece of writing, the resulting pieces are considerably longer. While the pieces are longer, they may also be more stilted due to this age group's attachment to using words they are sure they know how to spell. Figure 5.1 outlines many other changes that take place in writing growth over time for students in transition. Because of the range of writing abilities and rate of progress, individual children will reach a stage of transition at different ages. Teachers will find some writers in transition in first grade as well as in fourth grade.

One thing teachers notice when working with children in this age group is that they tend to take things literally (Calkins, 1994) and overgeneralize new learning. An example of taking things literally comes from

Figure 5.1   Change Over Time in Writing Development

	Early Elementary	Transition	Intermediate
Writing	• Uses basic narrative structure of familiar topics • Writes a few sentences • Uses simple sentence structure • Thinks consciously about forming words • Uses some conventional spellings of high-frequency words • Uses invented spellings of some complex words • Does little revision or editing • Does little conscious planning • Matches illustrations to text • Uses illustrations to inspire text • Labors to record a message	• Uses basic narrative structure with different topics • Begins to carry pieces over several days • Has variable use of end punctuation; experiments with other punctuation • Has control over a core of high-frequency words • Uses invented spelling of many complex words • Does some editing • Revises, but often limited to adding more text • Uses some planning • Supplements text with illustrations	• Makes deliberate decisions about form and genre • Writes longer pieces of several pages • Uses more complex sentence structures • Uses most end punctuation correctly; uses others variably (e.g., quotation marks, commas, ellipses) • Writes fluently, yet slows for difficult words • Spells most words correctly • Revises and edits • Gives feedback for revision to other writers • Plans writing • Is forming a sense of audience

a third grader. His first-draft writing was illegible, with most of the words spelled incorrectly. When Sarah wanted to confer with him, she told him she wanted to talk to him about his piece of writing but couldn't read it. Without skipping a beat, he said, "We were told that this was our sloppy copy, so I made sure to make it sloppy." That comment started her using the term "first best effort" with this literal age group! In another class, after several minilessons on the use of conversation in writing, several children used conversation to the exclusion of any narrative connections to the conversation or the accompanying quotation marks to note conversation. As can be seen in the writing of the second grader in Figure 5.2, she made sure to include children talking in her writing. However, she overgeneralized to the point of only using conversation in her writing.

Figure 5.2   Second Grader's Writing

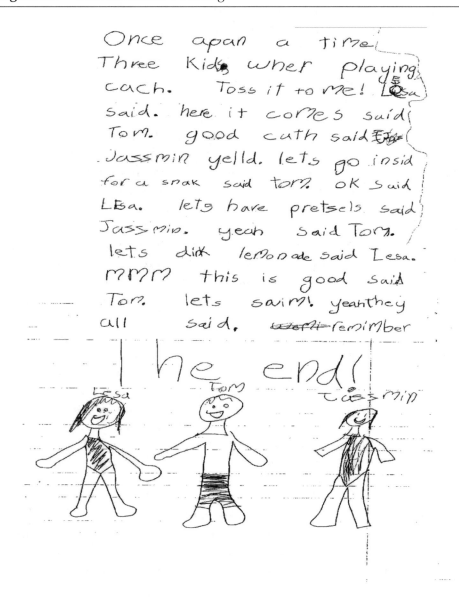

Children who are transitioning as writers will also respond to praise in their quest to "get it right." Graves (1983) talks about young writers reaching an "age of convention." At this "age" of learning, they understand there is a correct way to write, and they may lose the ability to explore writing and write with the abandon seen when they were younger. One of the major goals of writing instruction when children reach this "age" is to help them continue to stretch themselves as writers within this frame of desired correctness. How, then, do we do we make that happen in the classroom?

MAKING INSTRUCTIONAL DECISIONS

We have often been asked this question as well as other related ones: How do we meet the needs of the wide range of abilities and take into consideration the developmental needs of children? What instructional support for writing will be most helpful in moving all children forward as writers? How do we think about the levels of support writers need as a whole class, small groups, or individuals?

The best place to get started in answering these questions is to determine what the children are doing as writers and where they next need to go. Since there are differences in what children can do as writers, we need to analyze their independent attempts at writing to decide what lessons to teach. With the wide range of writing abilities in second and third grades, we need to assess students' writing and compare what these children can do as writers related to the district writing curriculum, state standards for writing, and standards for writing developed by various professional groups. An effective way to assess writing is to analyze one piece of writing each student drafted, revised, and edited independently to the best of his or her ability. Since most children at the early transition stage of writing may not be doing much editing and revising, it simply means they are handing in first-draft writing. Giving students the opportunity to reread what they have written allows them to be more thoughtful and do some checking. To meet the instructional goals for high-stakes writing assessments, teachers may also want to analyze writing children have completed related to a timed prompt, in order to determine what might need to be taught.

To effectively analyze student writing, you can prepare a grid (see Figure 5.3) to help organize and track what you are analyzing in the writing. It helps to attend to only a few things at a time so the task won't be so overwhelming. You may want to examine the writing with a state standard in mind or check on the independent use of an aspect of writers' craft and/or conventions you have been teaching. Sarah has worked with many teachers using this type of analysis for making teaching decisions. Figure 5.3 is an example that describes how it worked with one class.

Sarah chose to analyze personal narratives written by second graders in one class. She analyzed four things: organization (a recent focus in minilessons), staying on topic (a concern she noticed in conferences), including detail (a curricular focus she wanted to assess), and use of quotation marks

Figure 5.3   Class Analysis Grid

	Well Organized	Is Focused on Topic	Includes Interesting Details	Uses Quotation Marks Correctly	Notes
Meredith	X	X			No dialogue in this piece.
Kareem	X	X	X	X	
Helena	X	X		X	Has some detail but could improve.
Anita	X				* Lots of detail, lacks focus. No dialogue in this piece.
Korey			X		+*Work on organizing something already written.
Alex	X				*
Melissa	X				*
Rachel		X			+
Ruth	X	X		X	
Jana	X	X			
Stefanie	X	X			
Bryan					Needs more support. +*
José	X			X	Good use of dialogue. Needs more detail.
Quinton	X	X	X	X	Best work yet. Help him see this.
Blaze	X				*
Jasmine		X			+
Robin	X			X	
Yahira		X	X		+
Dawn	X				
Lisa	X	X		X	
Carmen	X				*
Aminah	X	X	X	X	
Mitchell	X				*

NOTES: + Guided-writing group on organization
*Guided-writing group on focus
Pieces in general were all quite short—mostly 3 to 4 sentences.

(a state standard and something she noticed students beginning to use). First, Sarah read each student's piece of writing, attending to organization, and put an X in the box for each student who demonstrated well-organized writing. This was an area she had been working on for some time, and she recognized that many children were now writing well-organized pieces, although they were rather short. Next, she reread each piece repeating the process, checking and recording students who successfully stayed on topic. She continued to repeat the process by rereading the papers each time she wanted to analyze something different in the writing. In this set of papers, she read each paper four times over the course of a week—one reading for each area of writing she wanted to analyze. While this seems time-consuming, Sarah was able to determine numerous instructional focuses for the whole class, small groups, and individuals that would last for several weeks.

By looking at the grid (Figure 5.3) for the spaces that did not have the X, Sarah was quickly able to determine that Korey, Rachel, Bryan, Jasmine, and Yahira still needed to work on organization. She thought about how to make that happen and decided to pull them together as a guided-writing group over several weeks during writing workshop.

Looking back at the chart, Sarah decided to focus her next set of mini-lessons to the whole class on staying on a single topic when writing. Only half the class seemed to be staying focused on a topic, so she determined more work for the whole group on this would be helpful. She decided to use shared writing to model and provide high support. Later, she would choose minilessons for the whole class to help students include interesting details in their writing. This was an area in which most students in the class needed instruction, but Sarah decided for now to keep this on hold. While this process of analysis took considerable time, it paid big dividends in generating lesson ideas that could be used for more than a month of writing instruction.

After analyzing student writing for use of dialogue, Sarah decided to highlight how dialogue is written in shared and guided reading, as a way to help more children begin to look closely at the use of quotation marks before bringing this convention into a writing workshop minilesson. Following a series of minilessons on detail, she could begin to focus minilessons on the use of quotation marks in dialogue. However, she decided to wait until more students showed awareness of quotation marks before teaching about them in whole-class minilessons for writing workshop.

Sarah also realized she needed to start working with students to expand their writing, a common need during transition. She decided to start this in individual conferences with children who were ready to do more than simply add to their written pieces, and recorded individual progress. She decided to assess this later in the year with the whole class to see whether more of them were ready for expanding their writing. She also thought she could begin to model ways for students to expand their written pieces during shared and interactive writing.

This method of analyzing children's writing makes it easy to see shifts we need to make in minilessons and what instructional tools might best meet the learning needs of children in the class. The grid helps focus our thinking and what we attend to when looking at student writing. This helps us see what children are doing independently as writers, how they are using what we have taught, and what we need to teach. By using assessment to determine the appropriate lessons for students and the most effective instructional tools, we are meeting children where they are and moving them forward, always mindful of standards and where students need to be as writers as they move into the intermediate grades.

To meet the diverse needs of writers, we want to consider the tools we use to teach writing in the primary grades and how the use of these tools changes as children transition into the intermediate grades. We use the term *instructional tools* to mean the contexts in which we can provide different levels of support. In teaching writing, there are shifts in levels of support needed as children develop as writers. There are also shifts in the use of tools for instruction used with the whole class, small groups, and children with specific needs.

MODELED WRITING

Modeled writing provides demonstrations on how writing works. It provides children with a window into the writing process. Since writing is often a solitary, silent act for experienced writers, it is important for children to see the process in action and hear the thoughts of a writer while writing is taking place. It is also important for children to engage in guided practice as they move toward independently applying what they know about writing. Modeled writing can range from high teacher support through demonstrations to shared and interactive writing, in which children participate in the writing process.

As teachers, we can provide high support through a modeling process by showing children how more experienced writers develop a piece of writing and by making our thoughts "visible" as we write. We can "think aloud" during the entire composition and transcription process to serve as a model for children. During transition, we focus mostly on modeling composition and the craft of writing because most children in transition are already comfortable getting words on paper. However, by making the process "visible" through our modeling, we can also focus on the transcription issues that cause some students to struggle. In addition to learning more about process, the high support of modeling and talking about our thinking provides opportunities for showing students how writing works in a variety of genres and for a variety of purposes.

SHARED WRITING

Shared writing is another form of modeled writing and can be used for introducing all aspects of writing children need to learn. In shared writing, the teacher and the children share in the oral composition of a piece of writing. The teacher is responsible for transcribing the message onto chart paper or an overhead transparency. In the example above, Sarah completed an assessment process and decided the class needed to work at staying on topic while composing text, and she chose shared writing as the tool to model this. She decided it was important to both show her own thinking and ask for student thinking when determining what would be on topic within a certain piece of writing. Shared writing provides opportunities to share these thought processes between the teacher and the class. Since the class was helping to compose the text, Sarah felt there would be opportunities to think through whether or not an idea would be helping the writing stay on topic.

Sarah's class completed a study of folktales and compared different versions of *Cinderella*. The class decided to write its own version and discussed what things were essential for this type of story. They decided there needed to be a person who was being picked on by a stepparent and siblings; there needed to be a magical being who made changes in the person's life; and there had to be someone to live with happily ever after. The class had previously been talking about how most of the tales had a problem to be solved and decided to determine the setting, character names, a problem, a solution, and details before writing. Once they had this frame for the writing, through shared writing, they made a list of things to include.

During the first day of shared writing, the plan was completed. Each day for 2 weeks, children in the class continued to brainstorm ideas to include in the story. The class checked each brainstormed idea proposed for inclusion in the story against the plan made on the first day to determine whether the idea fit within the focus. They were also able to continually reread what they had previously written to see whether it followed the story line or if they were being diverted from it. This shared-writing activity made it possible for the class to think aloud about what to add to the story that would stay within the stated focus.

By having models available, children can see how they need to think while they are writing, and teachers can refer to shared-writing charts to guide children as they grow into mature writers. The high support of modeling and talking about the process of writing while students can see it in action provides opportunities for teaching writing. There are many opportunities for shared writing beyond retellings and responding to literature. Shared writing can be used for introducing new craft or conventions in writing or a new genre, and it can be used for a variety of purposes and audiences (Routman, 2000). Shared writing can be used to write class thank-you notes, invitations, class newsletters, observations from experiments, reviews of field trips, poetry, story maps, and math charts and graphs (Routman, 2000).

INTERACTIVE WRITING

Another writing tool similar to shared writing and also a form of modeled writing is interactive writing. It can be used for similar purposes and

Figure 5.4   Planning List for *Cinderella* Shared Writing

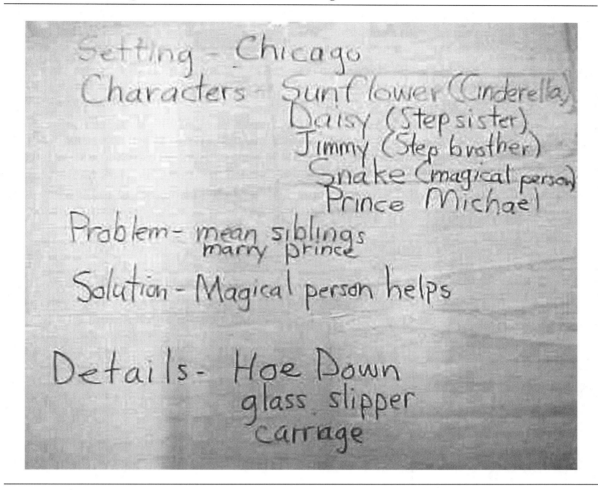

audiences as shared writing and is another way to model composition and construction through the active involvement of students. However, in interactive writing, there is less teacher support in that children have the opportunity to do some of the transcribing of the group writing. One important focus of interactive writing is emphasis on involving the children in constructing the text (McCarrier, Pinnell, & Fountas, 2000). This emphasis is important in the early primary grades to show children how to put their thoughts down on paper. Many teachers in second and third grades find their instructional focus is more on composition and that shared writing better meets their needs. However, we have found that there are times when teachers of writers in transition may want to have students do some writing on the chart to highlight something new they are learning. For example, in one second-grade classroom, the teacher was introducing the use of conversation in writing. She wanted the students to be clear about when to use commas and where to place the quotation marks. She decided to ask them to come up to the chart and add the commas and quotation marks themselves as a way to draw attention to the punctuation they needed to use when writing conversation. Another third-grade teacher found that her children needed more work on writing multisyllable words. As part of the transcription process, whenever these words came up during a modeled-writing lesson, she asked students to think of the words in syllables and asked one student to come to the chart to record the syllables of the word in order.

In the primary grades, children come to the chart most often to write letters or words. As children in transition become more adept at putting their messages on paper, the teacher may ask a student to act as scribe to write phrases, a sentence, or even several sentences while the class composes the piece. The teacher works with the rest of the class on developing the composition or on going into more detail related to the transcription process, taking over the task of writing to assist as needed or to keep the flow of the writing moving more quickly.

Interactive writing is useful with small groups of children in second and third grades who need more support and specific instruction. In the following example (Mahurt, 2005), the teacher started by reviewing a phonics lesson previously taught. She talked about consonant clusters and using consonant clusters when writing words. After negotiating the text and deciding on what to write, the class chose this sentence: "The seed turns into a sprout." Here's what took place at the point they were about to write the word *sprout:*

T:	Sprout. Sprout has parts you know.
S (several):	Out.
T:	Yes. Out. What about the consonant cluster?
S (several):	/spr/, /spr/, S-P-R. (One student writes "spr" on the chart, the teacher adds "out.")
	(More interactive writing took place to complete the sentence and add another.)
T:	(At the end of the lesson) Today, you listened for parts you know. When you write today, think about what you hear and what you know, like the consonant cluster in sprout. It will help you to use what you know when you are writing new words.

WRITING WORKSHOP

Writing workshop provides less support than the different forms of modeled writing. Writing workshop is the one time during the day when the whole class can be engaged in independent writing, while the teacher provides some support and meets the individual needs of students through writing conferences. This is an important time of day, since each child is working within his or her abilities, while at the same time growing as a writer. Writing workshop can include a combination of writing experiences that focus on assigned and self-selected writing in a variety of genres and content areas (Fountas & Pinnell, 2001). The structure of writing workshop is consistent from day to day, with a lesson focusing on an aspect of writing, followed by a writing time, in which children write independently and the teacher confers with individual writers or works with small groups, and a time for sharing.

The instructional contexts within writing workshop do not change over time as children get older, but the time spent writing in workshop and the instruction that takes place in the workshop change as children transition from the primary to intermediate grades. Writing workshop consists of three parts: a minilesson, time to independently write and confer with the teacher and each other, and time to share student work. Minilessons are 5 to 10 minutes long and focus on one aspect of writing, such as a convention, composition, revision, or editing strategy. The minilesson includes explicit instruction addressing what most members of the class need to learn. Following the minilesson, students write independently for 20 to 40 minutes. The time spent writing gradually increases as students are able to write for longer periods. During this independent writing time, the teacher confers individually with students on their particular needs as writers, or the teacher may bring together small guided- or interactive-writing groups when several children have a common issue that needs to be addressed. After the time spent in independent writing and conferring, some students share an entire piece or a section of their writing with the whole class, a small group, or a partner. Sharing time lasts about 10 to 15 minutes. Each element of the writing workshop is important, so in this chapter, we detail each of them, with a focus on the changes necessary as students transition into the intermediate grades.

MINILESSONS

As discussed previously in this chapter, assessing children's writing is the best way to determine the lessons children need. Once their strengths and needs are identified, explicit instruction in composing text and using conventions can take place through minilessons. However, it is useful to have a list of possible minilessons during transition to guide your thinking. Figure 5.5 lists some of those minilessons, arranged in four different categories. The first column on the chart lists some procedural minilessons you might use to help writing workshop function smoothly. Many of these procedures will have been discussed in the primary grades, but all students need reminders of procedures from time to time. The second column, on strategies, lists minilessons that highlight what writers do. This includes lessons such as how writers get ideas and what they do when they are stuck. Again, some of these lessons will have been introduced in the primary grades, but students who are writers in transition will continue to develop and need support in these areas. They will also need to improve in their ability to reread their writing with a focus on meaning, clarity, and organization. The third column, on composing/revising, lists lessons related to the craft of writing and includes genre and style. These lessons are revisited again and again as children continue to develop as writers. The fourth column consists of minilessons on language conventions. Once children master one aspect of the conventions, minilessons move forward to more complex skills. This is not an exhaustive list of minilessons, but represents some ideas to consider as you work with students in writing workshop. Shifts in writing minilessons for writers in transition are based on assessments to determine the strengths and needs of individual children, patterns of these needs among groups of children in the class, as well as the standards and writing curriculum for that grade level.

Figure 5.5   Possible Minilessons for Transitional Writers

Procedures	Strategies Writers Use	Composing/Revising	Conventions
• Using workshop time • Being a member of a writing community • Using and caring for writing materials • Using paper: what kind, one side, skipping lines • Using the writing folder • Keeping records of writing projects • Tracking what has been learned • Learning to respond to other writers	• Choosing topics: how writers get ideas • Using a writer's notebook • Sketching • Reading old pieces of writing for ideas • Cutting and pasting • Learning how to edit • Using editing marks • Avoiding plagiarism • Considering genres • Reading like a writer: using literature as a springboard • Rereading own writing for meaning, clarity, organization, etc.	• "Showing" the reader, not "telling" • Adding details to writing • Knowing when there are too many details • Using concise language • Using descriptive language: verbs, adverbs, adjectives • Writing effective leads • Writing effective endings • Using text structures for different purposes • Considering the audience • Focusing the writing	• Handling spelling concerns • Writing high-frequency words fluently • Using punctuation: quotation marks, commas, colons, apostrophes, etc. • Using resources: dictionary, thesaurus, word charts • Proofreading own writing • Using paragraphs • Understanding parts of speech • Using capital letters

SOURCE: Adapted from Fountas & Pinnell (2001); Avery (1993).

Once you determine what most of the class needs, you can think about ways to develop effective lessons. There are questions you can ask to guide your thinking as you prepare minilessons:

- How will I demonstrate what I want students to learn using clear and explicit language?
- How will I use examples from children's writing, my writing, or literature to show what I mean?
- How will I connect new learning to what children already know?
- How will I actively engage students in the lesson?
- How do these lessons connect to the curricula/standards that I need to teach?

The content of lessons is determined by the needs of most of the students in the class, keeping in mind the standards and curricula that also guide instructional decisions. Short, focused lessons with clear, explicit, and concise teaching points are most effective (Fountas & Pinnell, 2001). It is important to focus on one point in a lesson even when you know there are many other things you need to teach. Students can more easily attend to one new idea at a time and use it in their own writing.

INDEPENDENT WRITING AND CONFERRING

After the minilesson, the students write independently while the teacher confers individually with students or meets with small groups of students who have similar needs. This is the heart of writing workshop. Conferences with students are conversations about writing designed to develop content, form, or knowledge of being a writer. Sometimes, the purpose of the conference is to help writers evaluate their writing. At other times, conferences may be about editing. Conferences may also focus on the revision process. Calkins (1994) talks about the conference as the time when the teacher is guiding students' thinking so young writers can learn to "pull back from their pages and ask themselves questions that have been asked of them" (p. 222). The purpose of the conference is to move individual students into independence through the teachers' guiding questions— questions that will resonate inside children's heads as they write and reread their own writing.

The format of the writing conference remains the same as children get older. Teachers begin the conference by asking research questions to inform their decisions about what to teach during the conference (Anderson, 2000; Calkins, 1994). Once a decision is made, the teacher gives feedback and teaches the student something new and links it back to the independent writing the child is doing (Anderson, 2000).

In the following conference, the teacher begins by getting Meredith to talk about her work as a writer and guides her to look at the piece on which she is currently working:

Teacher: Meredith, can you show me what you are working on as a writer?

Meredith: I'm trying to get a beginning in my stories. . . . I think I am.

Teacher: Let's look at your story. Will you read me the beginning?

Meredith: I went to a field trip. We went to Healthworks.

The teacher guides Meredith to use the class resources (see Figure 5.6) as a way to check on herself and link to what the class has been learning. Once Meredith realizes something is missing, she sees a place to revise.

Figure 5.6   Class Chart for Beginning, Middle, and End

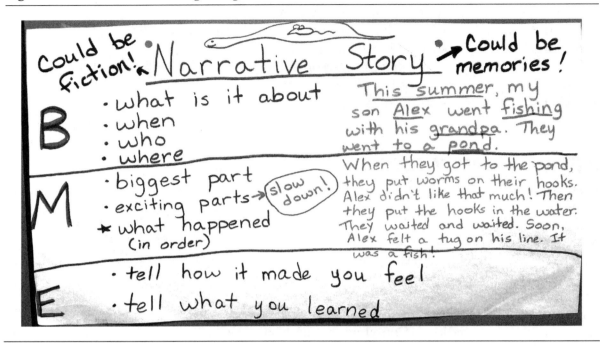

Teacher:	Let's check our chart to see what a beginning should have (reading from the chart). Hmmm, we need to make sure you tell what it is about.
Meredith:	A trip to Healthworks. I have that here.
Teacher:	Okay. Now, do you have when?
Meredith:	(rereads) I forgot that part.
Teacher:	So we know you need to put that in. Do you have the who and where?
Meredith:	Yeah. It was us and I said Healthworks.

In continuing the conference, the teacher guides Meredith to a bigger picture. She wants her to check her beginning and encourages her to use a chart the class developed for this purpose:

Teacher:	What can you do to check for yourself if you have all you need at the beginning of your writing?
Meredith:	I can look at the chart and see if I have everything there.

Once the teacher feels the student understands how to grow as a writer in the area being discussed—in this case, the beginning—a goal is set for the child's writing development. In the primary grades, the teacher writes the goal to keep a record of it. As children can write more fluently, they begin to write their own goals and keep them in their writing folders. This way, writers in transition participate in keeping track of what they are learning and how they are developing as writers.

There is a consistent structure to each conference, and over time students understand their roles in the conference. There is an expectation the student will lead at the beginning of a conference by talking about what he or she is working on as a writer. While the structure of the conference remains the same, the subject matter discussed changes over time. As children grow as writers, what they need to talk about in their writing conferences will change. Fletcher and Portalupi (2001) list some common conference topics and outline the changes from kindergarten to middle school. Their work shows that some K–1 conference topics will be centered around drawing; adding words to drawings; saying words slowly to hear sounds to write; spacing issues; and including a beginning, middle, and end to a story. These topics change in second through fourth grades, with much more focus on composition development. Possible conference topics during these transition years center on locating an important part on which to work, knowing when there is more than one story in a piece, managing a large topic, writing with the reader in mind, cutting and pasting, and developing a lead (Fletcher & Portalupi, 2001). The focus has changed from getting the writing down on paper to developing the writing that is already there.

While the teacher is working with individual children in conferences, the rest of the students are writing independently. In Chapter 1, we discussed the importance of children having time to work independently to practice what they have been taught. Writing workshop is a time for children to take what they are learning and try it on their own. Through other instructional opportunities, such as shared writing, students are supported through guided practice. Writing workshop is a time for independent practice. The writing children do, along with their actions and behaviors while independently writing, provides teachers with information about what students have learned and paths they are taking in becoming writers.

SHARING

Time for sharing student work is provided at the end of every writing workshop. Sharing presents opportunities for students to talk about their writing. One thing that changes as children transition is that they may no longer share entire pieces of writing with the whole class. Their writing is often too long and not compelling enough to hold the attention of a large group of listeners. It can also be very time-consuming to share entire pieces of writing to address only one small portion for new or reinforced learning. On some days, children may still share whole pieces with other students in small groups or with partners. This is important to do occasionally because children still enjoy and gain value from sharing their entire pieces of writing with others in the class.

During whole-group sharing time, children talk about concerns they have about their own writing—things they may want help with. They may share something they did as writers that would benefit the writing of other class members. The teacher's role in sharing is similar to that in conferences (Fletcher & Portalupi, 2001), to direct the learning and to model thinking for the writers, both when they are writing and when they are conferring. During sharing time, students can talk about and show how they used something from the minilesson in their writing. This is a powerful way to demonstrate that there is an expectation for learning something from the minilesson and then begin using it in students' writing.

Sharing time is for learning and also for celebration. Students may ask to share to get help or to celebrate a specific accomplishment. The teacher may ask students to share something discussed in a conference or something specific in someone's writing in order to reinforce or model learning for others in the class. For example, several students could share a lead they were working on and talk about how they made the decision to go with this particular lead. In one sharing session, Alex wanted to ask for help with an ending for his story. When he asked the teacher for help, she suggested he summarize and tell the class what he had written up to the point of his ending and then read only the ending for feedback from his classmates. Students suggested ways he might further develop his ending. One classmate asked whether he wanted a surprise ending. Since he had written a retelling of the story, *The Three Little Pigs,* someone else suggested he just close with "And they lived happily ever after." Alex wanted more ideas. The teacher suggested he might read the endings to different versions of the story to see whether that would give him ideas. Another student suggested he try writing several different endings to see which he liked best. Following sharing, Alex decided he would read some different endings and then try writing some for himself.

REFLECTION

When thinking about teaching writers in transition, it is important to keep in mind who they are as individual writers, what they know and need to know, and the established expectations of standards and curricula for their grade levels. It is also important to think about instructional tools and effective ways to use them to provide appropriate amounts of support to best meet the needs of all students as they learn new skills and strategies as writers.

6

Pulling It All Together

"I just don't know how I can fit it all in. I'm so overwhelmed." This is a common cry from classroom teachers who struggle to address state and local curriculum standards in all the content areas and deal with increasingly diverse students as they plan and deliver instruction that follows current research for best practice. Finding time in each day to address literacy, math, and content-area subjects is challenging, particularly as students move toward intermediate grades, where content areas are more heavily stressed. As teachers, we long to recreate the joy of teaching and learning with our students but often get bogged down by numerous demands and increasing expectations.

In this chapter, we first talk about integrating the language arts. Since there are reciprocal connections between learning to read and write (Mahurt, 2005), we can help children link these language processes. Whether teaching skills or teaching children how to take strategic action, it is important to carry the specific focus throughout the literacy block. This makes learning to read and write a more natural and successful experience. In addition to linking teaching within the language arts, Ruth shares a unit of study completed with her second graders in which she was able to link reading, writing, and word study while combining content learning in science and social studies.

In her book *Reading Essentials*, Regie Routman (2002) talks about "teaching with a sense of urgency" (p. 41). She is implying not that we need to put undue pressure on ourselves, but, rather, that we need to make our time for instruction really count. As we think about the needs of transitional readers and writers and our expectations, instruction should reflect our goal for them to use what they already know and are currently learning with increasing flexibility and independence.

Integrating instruction is one way to relieve the pressure of trying to fit everything into our busy instructional days. And the explicit linking of instruction makes learning much more powerful for students. When the lessons we teach and the activities we develop fit together, there is a more natural flow to instruction and increased learning. Children experience what it is like to be a lifelong learner, using what they know to learn new things. Students and teachers feel more relaxed and joyful as they go about the day's work. To make this happen, teachers will want not only to reflect on the needs of students in each area of literacy but also to think about how to guide them to connect and apply what they are learning. Teachers can get even more mileage out of this type of reflective planning when they consider how to weave science and social studies topics into their literacy instruction.

INTEGRATING WITHIN THE LANGUAGE ARTS

One of the links between reading and writing is composing a response to reading. As seen in previous chapters, this can easily be worked into minilessons in both reading and writing workshop. After some read-aloud sessions, we discuss our thinking about the books and record our thoughts. As we write together in a class reading log, many children ask whether they can write their own responses, either adding to the class reading log, as seen in Figure 6.1, or writing responses during writing workshop. These attempts can be used as examples for writing or reading minilessons, providing clear models that children perceive as being within their reach. Connecting their own reading and writing in lessons not only makes sense but also encourages all students to attempt something new by showing them how it has been done by one of their own classmates.

As children read longer text during guided-reading lessons, they can be encouraged to write longer texts as well. The type of language and sentence structure in books students are reading independently can be guides for types of language structures to encourage them to use in their writing. In late fall of second grade, one of Tanisha's students noticed the amount of time spent reading independently was close to the amount of time the class stayed focused on their writing during writing workshop. As children began to read chapter books, it was common for them to want to attempt writing chapter books. This was an early indication that students were beginning to become aware of the connection between their abilities as readers and writers. While writing chapter books is probably beyond the reach of most children in second and third grades, it is an indication that they are aware that longer text is often segmented and signals when we can begin to teach children to organize their writing into paragraphs, series of events, and collections.

Children also made a connection between reading and writing after one teacher read several chapter books to the class. Students began to

Figure 6.1   Class Reading Journal

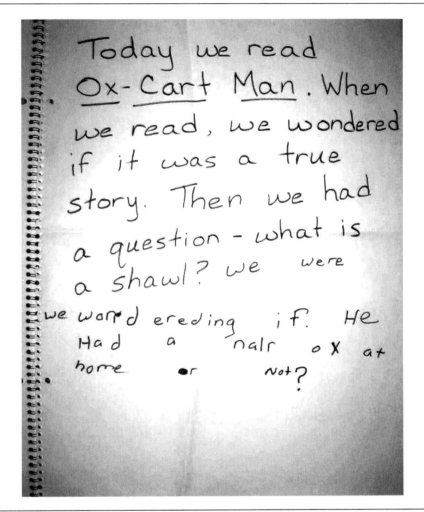

include a table of contents in their writing pieces or used one to organize collections of stories with similar topics. In response to several reading workshop minilessons on the structure of fairy tales and folktales, Candice became totally immersed in writing her own fairy tales about a series of princesses. After she had written several, she shared them with the class, sparking a review of what had previously been learned about writing narrative text and how fairy tales fit into that genre. Candice's princess stories were published in the classroom as a collection, and she made sure to include a table of contents, as can be seen in Figure 6.2. Students were able to do these things because the class spent a lot of time noticing and discussing text features and genres, with the teacher deliberately making her own thinking visible to students and modeling how they could use various text features in their own writing.

Even comprehension strategy lessons can be easily connected to writing. The class learned about using clues in the texts they were reading to

Figure 6.2 Student's Table of Contents

help them infer how characters were feeling. Using examples they found as models, they also learned how to use clues in their own stories that would help readers know about the characters. Charts of pictures and phrases that supported inferences covered a wall, tracking the work of the students as readers. The class searched for places in text where they had to infer how a character felt. Finding phrases and picture clues to support their inferences helped the children develop deeper comprehension and provided models for their own writing. In following the students' interests, writing workshop minilessons focused on using language that would help the reader infer how characters felt without saying it directly. Lindsey, while writing about a trip to an amusement park, changed part of her story in response to this study on characters. Instead of merely saying she was scared on a large ride, she stated, "My eyes got really big."

In addition, word study authentically fit with reading and writing workshop lessons as the students in class learned about using more varied, precise vocabulary in their writing. Since inferences are often dependent upon descriptive phrases to "show" the reader instead of "telling," lessons on descriptive words and synonyms supported the children's efforts as writers. The discussions and study about using words and phrases to infer while reading not only helped students comprehend at a deeper level but also piqued their interest in finding new ways to move forward as writers.

In a writing workshop minilesson in third grade (Mahurt, 2005), Kristin reread the descriptive language from several books she had previously read aloud to the children. One of the books, *Red Dancing Shoes* (Patrick, 1993), described the shoes that had gotten dirty as "blotchy and muddy and sticky" (n.p.). The class talked about the meaning of *blotchy* and how the author made the image of the dirty shoes come alive. Kristin charged the children to use more colorful language in their own writing. This discussion about word meaning not only helped them learn a word but also interested them in finding new words in their reading and words they could use in their writing.

Using whole-class or individual pieces of writing as material for minilessons in text reading is another way teachers can link reading and writing. For example, using interactive- or shared-writing pieces to practice attending to punctuation and phrasing helps children become more fluent readers, particularly since it gives them a chance to practice the new learning on a text familiar to them while being supported by the teacher. The teacher provides high support in these whole-class sessions and can refer to these experiences as he or she moves into guided-practice opportunities during guided-reading lessons and independent-reading conferences.

Finding ways to integrate word study with reading and writing can be challenging, but it is important to link the isolated word work to reading and writing of whole texts. For example, Greg, a third-grade teacher, linked his study of digraphs to reading and writing. During shared-reading sessions and guided-reading lessons, the class looked for consonant digraphs when solving unknown words, which supported students' use of these patterns to solve words in more independent settings. During writing workshop time, children were encouraged to say words carefully and use the patterns they were learning for sounds such as /sh/or/th/. Finally, words being solved in reading and writing were collected on charts and used later for further word study.

INTEGRATING LANGUAGE ARTS WITH SCIENCE AND SOCIAL STUDIES

Content areas can be woven into literacy instruction, making more efficient and powerful use of time. Using reading and writing to learn new things is "real life" learning. Using read-aloud times, particularly if the read aloud is interactive, is a perfect time to introduce new content material. Many trade books are excellent sources of information, along with textbooks or big books used as read-aloud or shared-reading material. Newspapers printed specifically for children, such as *Time for Kids, Scholastic News,* and *Weekly Reader,* are another useful source of content-area reading for many schools. Readers in transition are ready and eager to be introduced to these types of text and can be supported as needed while moving toward independent reading in a new genre.

Teachers can link content-area read alouds and shared reading to inter-active- and shared-writing activities, while addressing science and social studies topics, by having children work together to create "Know," "Want to Know," and "Learned" (KWL) charts (Ogle, 1986) and recording new learning in a whole-class learning log. Children can keep personal logs to record content-area knowledge during workstations and during indepen-dent reading time. These types of activities provide writers in transition with new and authentic purposes for writing and help prepare them for note taking in intermediate grades.

In Ruth's second-grade classroom, she continually thinks about how learning can be connected for students to support and make integrating much easier for children's learning. Her nonfiction project illustrates how teachers can connect standards from several curriculum areas to make teaching more powerful. Ruth will lead us through her thought process as she combined what she knew about the strengths and needs of the children in her class, the state standards, and her prior instruction to plan and teach nonfiction through a science curriculum focus on ecosystems. As she considered the shifts being made by these learners, she sought oppor-tunities for them to use what they had previously learned and searched for ways to build on their strengths to scaffold current learning.

PLANNING THE NONFICTION PROJECT

This project began with a study of nonfiction in reading but rapidly grew to include all areas of language arts as well as science and social studies. Ruth's second graders were expected to not only read nonfiction but also use many features found in nonfiction text. They needed to be able to use a table of contents and an index, read charts and graphs, and understand simple diagrams. Ruth pulled several nonfiction titles from her classroom library and checked out several more from the school library, intending to use them for read alouds and shared-reading experiences. To provide more specific support navigating nonfiction text, she frequently chose nonfiction books for guided-reading groups. As children began to be exposed to more nonfiction titles, they seemed to burst with enthusiasm. Requests came fast and furious for books about dinosaurs, racecars, and exotic ani-mals. The classroom was energized, and Ruth began to think of ways to use this energy in other parts of the curriculum and the school day.

After looking at state and local curriculum standards, Ruth quickly realized there were rich opportunities for integration with the planned non-fiction study. Figure 6.3 outlines the state standards addressed in this unit of study. In addition, for example, students in the district were to learn characteristics of simple expository text and write informational pieces. They were also expected to plan and present brief speeches in order to share their collected information with others. The literacy pieces seemed to fall into place naturally. Ruth also saw many opportunities to expand vocabulary, something especially valuable for the English language learners in her classroom.

Figure 6.3   Indiana State Standards Used in Ecosystem Study

ECOSYSTEM STUDY: INDIANA STATE STANDARDS

Science

- 2.1.5 Demonstrate the ability to work with a team but still reach and communicate one's own conclusions about findings.
- 2.4.1 Observe and identify different external features of plant and animals and describe how these features help them live in different environments.
- 2.4.2 Observe that and describe how animals may use plants, or even other animals, for shelter and nesting.
- 2.4.4 Recognize and explain that living things are found almost everywhere in the world and that there are somewhat different kinds in different places.

Social Studies

- 2.3.1 Use cardinal and intermediate directions to locate places on maps and places in the classroom, school, and community.
- 2.3.3 Locate the local community and the United States on maps and globes.
- 2.3.5 Identify map symbols for land and water forms and give examples of these physical features in the local community.
- 2.3.7 Use a variety of information resources to identify ways that the physical environment influences human activities in the community.

Reading

- 2.2.11 Demonstrate an awareness of the sounds that are made by different letters by clearly pronouncing blends and vowel sounds.
- 2.2.1 Use titles, tables of contents, and chapter headings to locate information in text.
- 2.2.2 State the purpose for reading.
- 2.2.3 Use knowledge of the author's purpose to comprehend informational text.
- 2.2.4 Ask and respond to questions to aid comprehension about important elements of informational texts.
- 2.2.5 Restate facts and details in the text to clarify and organize ideas.
- 2.2.7 Interpret information from diagrams, charts, and graphs.

Writing

- 2.4.2 Organize related ideas together to maintain a consistent focus.
- 2.4.4 Understand the purposes of various reference materials (such as a dictionary, thesaurus, or atlas).
- 2.5.2 Write a brief description of a familiar object, person, place, or event that develops a main idea; use details to support the main idea.
- 2.5.6 Write for different purposes and to a specific audience or person.
- 2.6.9 Spell correctly words with short- and long-vowel sounds, r-controlled vowels, and consonant-blend patterns.

Speaking and Listening

- 2.7.1 Determine the purpose or purposes of listening (such as to obtain information, to solve problems, or to enjoy).
- 2.7.5 Organize presentations to maintain a clear focus.
- 2.7.6 Speak clearly and at an appropriate pace for the type of communication (such as an informal discussion or a report to class).
- 2.7.9 Report on a topic with supportive facts and details.
- 2.7.11 Report on a topic with facts and details, drawing from several sources of information.

SOURCE: Reprinted with permission from The Indiana Department of Education.

Next, Ruth thought about how word study could support the children as they looked for information in their nonfiction texts. After skimming through several of the titles, she realized they would need to be able to apply what they had learned about decoding multisyllable words, especially using long-vowel patterns. This was a wonderful opportunity to review the patterns they had studied up to this point in the year. It also allowed Ruth to combine the review with strategies for problem solving unknown words with more than one syllable. Tying the review and practice to an authentic task would enable them to link word study to their independent reading. With the focus on applying what they had learned, Ruth set the expectation that the decoding skills learned during word study time would be used to decode words encountered in nonfiction text.

Next, Ruth turned her attention to science and social studies. Fitting these content areas into the fabric of each day was always difficult, but weaving them into literacy learning made sense. Although Ruth was typically in the habit of using literacy time to address science and social studies topics, she was surprised to find that by looking at the standards with more deliberate, intentional thought, it became possible to completely integrate the learning. In second grade, students needed to learn basic map skills, locate places on the globe, and learn how people in different places may live differently. In addition, they needed to explore the basic elements of various ecosystems and think about how plants and animals are suited to their systems. Within a short period of time, Ruth quickly found that state standards (see Figure 6.3) and local curriculum combined neatly into one nonfiction study.

This study was quickly becoming much more powerful and far-reaching than Ruth had originally planned. It is extremely important for learners in transition to continue developing independence with increasingly complex tasks. She had been working all year to step back and encourage students to try things out on their own as they became more confident and competent as readers and writers. The students were clearly ready to tackle this nonfiction study and use what they were learning about literacy to help them learn in content areas. Her goal was to continue developing opportunities for them to take on more responsibility for their learning, providing support only when necessary.

PREPARING FOR THE NONFICTION PROJECT

Ruth began preparations for instruction by collecting many titles on various ecosystems. It was important to include titles that represented a range of difficulty similar to the reading levels of the students—everything from Elaine Landau's *Grassland Mammals* (1996) to Gail Gibbons's *Nature's Green Umbrella: Tropical Rain Forests* (1994) to Elizabeth Tayntor's *Dive to the Coral Reefs* (1986). Students worked hard up to this point in the year to be able to choose just-right books, and this task was one most of these readers in transition had mastered. As in most classrooms, Ruth had a range of abilities and wanted each child to be able to find a book that was accessible. She and her students had also engaged in extensive work on what readers do prior to reading a text, so these readers were competent at introducing new books to themselves. Ruth also made sure to include some fiction stories, such as *The Great Kapok Tree,* by Lynn Cherry (1990), for each ecosystem. She knew many of her readers still needed some support and practice in identifying and navigating unfamiliar genres. This would allow for practice with peer groups in sorting books by genre. She also wanted to provide students with an opportunity to practice adjusting their approaches to text, since this is another skill most readers in transition are able to handle at this point in their learning.

To prepare for the nonfiction study, Ruth put books into baskets sorted by ecosystem, added a folder with sticky notes that students could use to mark places of interest in their texts, and added blank paper for recording information. Beside each basket was a sheet of paper with spaces for three to four children to write their names. When the children arrived the next morning, they immediately started browsing through baskets and talking excitedly about the various books they found intriguing. They determined their own study groups and signed up to research an ecosystem. At this point, the class had not studied specific ecosystems as a group. Instead of leading this study, Ruth decided that students would work with their peers, using their knowledge of reading, writing, and word solving to engage with the topic. This allowed them to apply what they knew independently in a less teacher-supported setting.

LITERACY LESSONS ON NONFICTION

Reading minilessons began by independent exploration on nonfiction text, specifically, how nonfiction text differs from fiction and why readers need to be aware of which kind of text they are reading. The children worked together as a class to create lists of various types of nonfiction text and reasons why readers might choose to read this genre. For example, they decided to include "how-to" pieces and stated that people often need to read how to do something (i.e., follow a recipe or create a craft project). Students already had numerous personal experiences with this type of reading. The art teacher often wrote directions on how to recreate a special project for use as follow-up, independent work for students in the classroom. This increased awareness of nonfiction made it seem more accessible for reading. Also, during reading workshop that week, children made sure to include books from the ecosystem baskets in their independent reading. As a review and quick observational assessment opportunity, Ruth asked them to bring these books to the debriefing time after the workshop and shared which titles were fiction and which were nonfiction.

While the children were working with nonfiction during reading time, writing workshop had a similar focus. Some minilessons centered on how expository text is organized and others on writing information pieces. Ruth used some of the easier texts from the ecosystems collection as examples. A few early minilessons involved shared-writing activities designed to support children in thinking about a piece before beginning to write. Since students were still in the early stages of learning about ecosystems, their attempts at this genre were about things they already knew. Parker, for example, had a collection of model trains in his basement, and he began to write about different types of trains. Brodie, who had previously been afraid of spiders, read about them and decided to write a book about spiders to help others understand that spiders weren't so scary after all. As they learned more about ecosystems, the information started appearing in several students' independent writing.

To support the challenge of more complex words showing up in their reading, word study sessions began with a review of what children already knew related to solving new words. During whole-group word work, Ruth was able to model possible word-solving strategies and share the task with the children as they worked together in shared-reading pieces solving new words. During one lesson, Ruth used a big book about the African desert. As they came to difficult words in the text, children gave suggestions for solving the unknown words and also for checking the success of their attempts. They quickly found that looking letter by letter was not only a slow approach but also meant they had to make more adjustments as they went along. In no time, the children agreed that looking through the word "in order" (from left to right) while scanning for larger "chunks" was a smarter way to approach unknown words. Ruth was able to follow up and refer to these shared experiences in small-group and individual learning settings, enabling her to adjust the level of support needed by various students in the class.

When the children came to the guided-reading table, they had a chance to try out the strategies with teacher support readily available when needed. As Ruth conferred with children during independent reading, she was able to see how individuals dealt with unknown words and how they applied learning from whole-group and small-group instruction. Watching individuals and small groups during this time gave her valuable feedback in knowing whether more whole-group instruction was necessary or whether small-group or individual instruction was more appropriate. The explicit link between reading and word study enabled students to understand that their work with words did not stand alone, but was connected to their own reading across the school day. Ruth knew students were being successful and making connections the day Brodie announced, "Hey, I read that word I didn't know fast! I did like we said after lunch [our word study time]. I looked right through it and saw parts I knew, and then all of the [sic] sudden, I knew that word after all!"

As the children began to use what had been discussed in word study sessions, Ruth planned a few lessons designed to help them use the same principles in their writing. As a class, they thought about some words they wanted to use in shared writing and applied what they knew about solving difficult words in text reading as a way to attempt writing them. In one piece written together by Ruth and the class on how to brush teeth, students applied some things they knew about long-vowel sounds on words like *teeth* and *clean*, engaging in a perfect opportunity to refine their current knowledge. For example, the word *teeth* was needed for the story, and some children wanted to use "ee" to record the "long e" sound, while others were sure it was "ea." Still more thought that "e consonant e" was the way to go. Ruth showed the children how to write the word using each letter combination and then look to see if one "looked right." They immediately chose the right combination of letters, and in doing so learned a strategy for independently solving words when writing. Shared writing and independent writing during writing workshop provided Ruth with many additional opportunities for varied support and practice with individual students. Observing their attempts in their independent writing provided her with evidence that they were indeed applying what had been worked on in the lesson and they were being successful applying the strategies independently.

After several days of studying nonfiction during literacy time, students were ready to dig into learning about ecosystems. They were confident in their ability to handle new text and anxious to learn about their chosen ecosystems. On most days, the class had a short block of time devoted to science or social studies, and Ruth quickly designated those blocks as the primary time for work on their ecosystem projects. On days when this was not possible, parts of reading and writing time were used for reading and note taking in their ecosystem books. Although Ruth was initially hesitant to use reading and writing instructional time for this purpose, it quickly became obvious that it allowed children to connect and apply their learning about reading and writing nonfiction with science and social studies content. Not only is this a more authentic learning setting, but the link between literacy knowledge and pursuing knowledge in content areas is key for learners in transition as they move toward more content-driven curricula in the intermediate grades.

As the work of learning about ecosystems intensified, Ruth observed that the class needed minilessons on how to use various features of nonfiction texts, such as a table of contents, headings, and captions. She planned a whole-group lesson and asked the children about the features they were encountering in their texts. On a chart, they recorded the name of the feature, where to locate it in the text, and how it helped them understand what they were reading. Figure 6.4 is the chart the class developed. The class reading log was used to chart what they found, giving them a chance to share the task of responding to their reading.

Ruth often referred to the class chart during reading instruction in whole-group, small-group, and individual settings. As children gained control over using various features in nonfiction text to support their understanding, several also attempted to record features independently in their own reading logs. Their logs began to reflect the features they were most often encountering and using during their individual reading.

It was also evident from Ruth's observations that there was a need for minilessons on recording important information. As the children worked in their ecosystem groups to read the texts provided, she noticed that they were finding many things about the ecosystems they were studying but

Figure 6.4 Nonfiction Features Chart

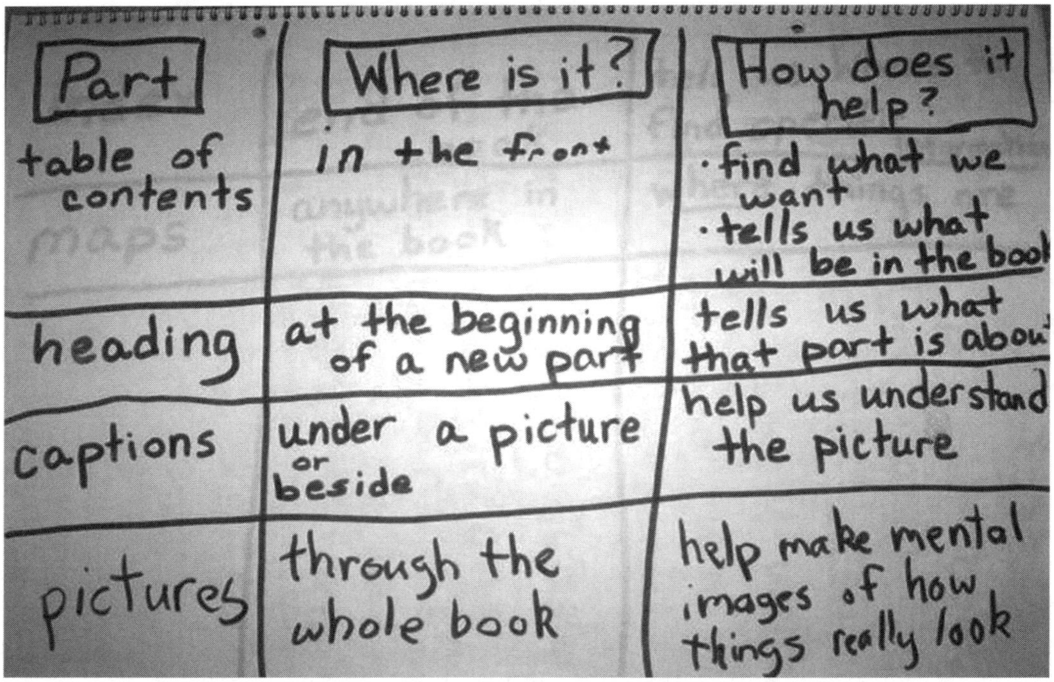

Part	Where is it?	How does it help?
table of contents	in the front	• find what we want • tells us what will be in the book
heading	at the beginning of a new part	tells us what that part is about
captions	under or beside a picture	help us understand the picture
pictures	through the whole book	help make mental images of how things really look

they were not writing anything down. She had provided each group with a folder containing blank paper for recording information, but they had no idea what they should be doing with the paper. Most groups were simply trying to remember all they learned, instead of writing or drawing what they were learning. During writing workshop, Ruth decided to focus on ways to record learning—a broader topic than simply note taking. As part of those minilessons, she and the class took notes together on texts read aloud or on nonfiction pieces read during shared reading. One book was about dragonflies. They read the book together, stopping at the end of each section to decide on the most interesting thing they had learned in that section. Then, they individually either wrote a sentence or drew a picture to record this learning. While working through this process, several children began to realize that recording interesting information in writing made it easier to later share the information with others. Brandon even suggested hanging notes in the hall, stating his concern, "There may be other kids who don't know this stuff, and we could help them!"

As the children began to realize how helpful it was to write down information, the ecosystem groups started to work together to record things they had learned from the books they were using. They also began to realize that some information could be found in more than one book, and some groups began to make marks next to information found in more than one text. They decided that if they found the same bit of information in several books, it must be important to remember. One group, in which the children had divided the texts to be read, used sticky notes to mark information they wanted to write down and then had group-sharing sessions to make sure they weren't duplicating information in their notes. The children were not only supporting each other in navigating nonfiction texts but also helping each other record their learning.

As Ruth observed children taking notes during project work times and talked with them during reading conferences or guided-reading lessons, another common need surfaced: the majority of students were struggling to identify which information was most important in the texts being read. Reading minilessons and practice at the guided-reading table were designed to quickly address this need, and she was able to check with individual readers as to what extent they were able to determine important ideas when reading on their own. During one guided-reading lesson, Ruth showed one group how to look at the heading for a section in nonfiction text about bats and use it to help them consider what the author viewed as being important to remember. After deciding what they thought was important, the children recorded information on sticky notes and stuck them to a large piece of paper. Over the course of the week, Ruth turned over responsibility for finding important information to children in the group. They started coming to group with notes prepared to share, and Ruth guided them to explain why they thought a particular piece of information was important.

Lessons about determining importance were mirrored during writing workshop. Ruth asked students to use what they learned about finding important information in books to guide them in deciding what was important to include in their writing. They eagerly began to discuss what kinds of information they would need to share with each other at the end of the ecosystem study. One group excitedly shared their idea of labeling sheets of paper to make sure important information was included in the final group projects. Soon, every group had pages labeled "animals," "plants," and "weather." The children also decided each group was responsible for using labeled sticky notes to mark places on the globe, showing where their ecosystems could be found. Children in the class were able to apply what they had learned to new situations and even expand on it. Their growing independence led to more excitement as the study of ecosystems continued.

With the focus of the work now more closely linked to the study of ecosystems, Ruth began to think again about word study and strategies she noticed children using when attempting to read or write new words on their own. What she observed was quickly confirmed by a spelling inventory (Bear, Invernizzi, Templeton, & Johnston, 2003). Most children in the class were correctly using consonant clusters and digraphs. They were using long-vowel patterns in their writing. While they used combinations to represent the correct sound, they often did not use the correct spelling pattern. In addition, many were beginning to make attempts at other, more complex vowel patterns. Ruth decided that word study lessons needed to revisit long-vowel patterns and begin to address other complex vowel patterns as well.

As the children explored the ecosystems texts, they were starting to pay attention to words that included the vowel patterns being studied during the word study block. Ruth and the children started to list some of the words and discussed how the words could be sorted. By using words they encountered in their reading, she helped students realize that spelling patterns they studied could help them solve words when reading. The linking of reading, writing, and word study through deliberate instruction within content areas seemed to be working. Students began to recognize the reciprocity between reading and writing by applying what they learned about one aspect of literacy to help them in another. Without even knowing it, they were taking important steps toward becoming more independent, flexible learners: a critical transition for children moving from primary to intermediate grades.

As the study began to wind down, Ruth talked with students about ways of sharing their learning. The students decided they would create posters, using drawings and writing to demonstrate their understandings. One group's poster is shown in Figure 6.5. The groups had several class sessions to create and practice with their posters, so when they presented to the rest of the class, the poster was used only as a guide for their presentation.

Following the presentations, the children decided others in the school might be interested in what they had learned. This resulted in the posters

Figure 6.5   Group Ecosystem Poster

being placed on display outside the classroom. The daily literacy block ended that day with sharing, a time that provided the opportunity to discuss what they had learned and to reflect on their own learning process. After the children had a chance to share their thoughts, it was Ruth's turn. She solemnly listed all they had learned and could do for themselves as a result of their work during this project. Their eyes grew wide and their mouths dropped as they realized just how much they had accomplished. As Ruth finished, Lindsey spoke up. "I don't think we could have done that at the beginning of the year!" She had hit the nail on the head. The shifts made by these children were indeed remarkable and worthy of much celebration.

This study lasted three weeks during the late spring. However, the amount of learning that took place during that time was tremendous. As much as possible, Ruth let the children do the work. She was an observer, available to step in and provide support, but only if needed. Her teaching decisions were based on what she noticed children attempting during independent work time rather than what she wanted them to learn or accomplish. She created or found numerous opportunities for linking literacy learning and applying it in content areas. For learners in transition, the ability to use the reciprocal links between reading, writing, and word study as a way to engage in content-area learning across the school day is vital to their success as they move into the more complex challenges of the intermediate grades.

REFLECTION

Successfully integrating learning in reading, writing, and word study while working in content areas often seems an insurmountable task. This is especially true at a time when teachers already feel pressured by increasing curriculum loads, high-stakes testing, and hard-to-reach learners. Interestingly, as the examples in this chapter make clear, it is through that very linking of instruction that the pressure can be relieved. Learning can become more meaningful, and teachers will be accomplishing more in less time. Not only does integrating ease the time burden for teachers, it creates more powerful learning opportunities for students. Integration of curriculum, especially when including science and social studies content, also helps to prepare transitional learners for the unique demands that await them in the intermediate grades.

Afterword

As we prepared to write this book, our goal was to provide a resource for our colleagues working with children in transition from primary to intermediate grades. While we certainly hope we have done that, we realize that what is contained within these pages reflects what we know now and that our knowledge is continually shifting. We will continue to observe children and teachers and grow in our thinking about how we might support literacy teaching and learning, and we hope that you will do the same.

What can teachers do to support literacy learners as they transition from primary to intermediate grades? Over the course of our work, several themes kept emerging and guided both the content and spirit of the book. The guiding themes are as follows: know your learners, make appropriate shifts in instruction, and guide all children to independence. While they are not all-encompassing, we believe they will serve teachers well.

KNOW YOUR LEARNERS

Although we focus on children in second and third grades, we realize that within the walls of our classrooms, learners represent a broad range of literacy development. Many children enter the transitional stage of literacy learning in late first grade, while others may not reach this stage until fourth or fifth grade. As teachers, it is important to realize that while many children follow a predictable pattern of literacy growth from grade to grade, it is more important to know where on the continuum of literacy development our students lie than it is to focus on specific grade levels. Having a sense of when children are ready to make a shift in literacy instruction grows out of learning to be sensitive observers and careful recorders of student processes and student work. This is what will enable us to meet the needs of all children.

SHIFTS IN INSTRUCTION

As children move beyond early literacy strategies, it makes sense that the content of literacy instruction will change, often becoming more complex in terms of challenges and expectations. What we must also remember is that the format of our instruction will shift as well. Our students will spend more and more time engaged in reading and writing continuous text and need opportunities for building stamina as readers and writers. Understanding how literacy learners are changing at this stage helps guide instruction, just as careful observation informs us as to when we need to make these instructional shifts. Linking reading, writing, and content areas through explicit instruction that sets clear expectations for students to use what they know is also essential in helping children make the shift from primary to intermediate grades. Powerful learning takes place when we teach for literacy learning across our day, not only in isolated blocks.

TEACH FOR STRATEGIC INDEPENDENCE

As odd as it may sound, our goal as teachers should be for children to not need us. Through the use of gradual release of responsibility, we move students toward independent problem solving so they have the strategies and confidence they need to take on tasks that are increasingly more complex. We also want our students to be strategic learners who apply what they know to new situations. Our instructional support varies in relation to student abilities and the demands of the tasks they face. Providing explicit whole-group instruction and numerous opportunities for shared and guided practice and gently moving children to independent practice allows them to take on the knowledge and abilities they will need to succeed in intermediate grades.

REFLECTION

We believe teachers must continually examine their instructional practices and make adjustments in response to shifts in student learning. It is our hope that this book provides teachers with a deeper understanding of the needs of children in transition between primary and intermediate grades, along with practical suggestions for how thoughtful instruction can build bridges for literacy learners moving from primary to intermediate grades. At the beginning of this book, we invited you to join us as we continue to learn more about ways we might support literacy learners as they grow and change. We hope the journey up to this point has stretched your understanding and has led you to examine and develop your instructional practices. We especially hope you will continue working to build bridges so that all children move forward as competent, confident readers and writers.

References

Alexander, P. (2005/2006). The path to competence: A lifespan developmental perspective on reading. *Journal of Literacy Research, 37,* 413–436.

Allington, R. (2000). *What really matters for struggling readers: Designing research-based programs.* Boston: Allyn & Bacon.

Anderson, C. (2000). *How's it going?* Portsmouth, NH: Heinemann.

Armbruster, B. B., Lehr, F., & Osborn, J. (2001). *Put reading first: The research building blocks for teaching children to read.* Jessup, MD: National Institute for Literacy.

Ash, G. E. (2002, March). Teaching readers who struggle. *Reading Online, 5*(7). Retrieved Jun 24, 2005, from http://www.readingonline.org/articles/art_index.asp?HREF=ash/index.html

Avery, C. (1993). *. . . And with a light touch.* Portsmouth, NH: Heinemann.

Bear, D. R., Invernizzi, M., Templeton, S., & Johnston, F. (2003). *Words their way* (3rd ed.). Upper Saddle River, NJ: Pearson Education.

Beaver, J. (1997). *Developmental reading assessment.* Parsippany, NJ: Celebration Press.

Beck, I. L., McKeown, M. G., & Kucan, L. (2002). *Bringing words to life: Robust vocabulary instruction.* New York: Guilford.

Booth, D. (1999). Language delights and word play: The foundation for literacy learning. In I. C. Fountas & G. S Pinnell (Eds.), *Voices on word matters: Learning about phonics and spelling in the literacy classroom* (pp. 91–102). Portsmouth, NH: Heinemann.

Calkins, L. (1994). *The art of teaching writing.* Portsmouth, NH: Heinemann.

Cappellini, M. (2006). Using guided reading with English learners. In T. A. Young & N. L. Hadaway (Eds.), *Supporting the literacy development of English learners* (pp. 113–131). Newark, DE: International Reading Association.

Clay, M. (2001). *Change over time in children's literacy development.* Portsmouth, NH: Heinemann.

Clay, M. M. (2002). *An observation survey of early literacy achievement* (2nd ed.). Portsmouth, NH: Heinemann.

Cunningham, P. M. (1999). *Phonics they use* (3rd ed.). New York: Allyn & Bacon.

DeFord, D. (2001). *Reading and writing assessment portfolio.* Carlsbad, CA: Dominie Press.

Diller, D. (2003). *Literacy work stations: Making centers work.* Portland, ME: Stenhouse.

Duke, N. K., & Pearson, P. D. (2002). Effective practices for developing reading comprehension. In A. E. Farstrup & S. J. Samuels (Eds.), *What research has to say about reading instruction* (3rd ed., pp. 205–242). Newark, DE: International Reading Association.

Fletcher, R., & Portalupi, J. (2001). *Writing workshop: The essential guide.* Portsmouth, NH: Heinemann.

Fountas, I. C., & Pinnell, G. S. (1996). *Guided reading: Good first teaching for all children.* Portsmouth, NH: Heinemann.

Fountas, I. C., & Pinnell, G. S. (2001). *Guiding readers and writers: Grades 3–6.* Portsmouth, NH: Heinemann.

Fountas, I. C., & Pinnell, G. S. (2003). *Phonics lessons: Letters, words, and how they work, Grade 2.* Portsmouth, NH: Heinemann.

Fountas, I. C., & Pinnell, G. S. (2006). *Leveled books K–8.* Portsmouth, NH: Heinemann.

Graves, D. (1983). *Writing: Teachers and children at work.* Portsmouth, NH: Heinemann.

Johnston, P. H. (2004). *Choice words.* Portland, ME: Stenhouse.

Kear, D. J., Coffman, G. A., McKenna, M. C., & Ambrosio, A. L. (2000). Measuring attitude toward writing: A new tool for teachers. *Reading Teacher, 54,* 10–23.

Keene, E., & Zimmerman, S. (1997). *Mosaic of thought.* Portsmouth, NH: Heinemann.

Mahurt, S. (2005). Writing is reading. *Indiana Reading Journal, 37,* 19–26.

McCarrier, A., Pinnell, G. S., & Fountas, I. C. (2000). *Interactive writing.* Portsmouth, NH: Heinemann.

McCormack, R. L., Paratore, J., & Dahlene, K. F. (2003). Establishing instructional congruence across learning settings: One path to success for struggling third-grade readers. In R. L. McCormack & J. R. Paratore (Eds.), *After early intervention, then what? Teaching struggling readers in Grades 3 and beyond* (pp. 117–136). Newark, DE: International Reading Association.

McKenna, M. C., & Kear, D. J. (1990). Measuring attitudes toward reading: A new tool for teachers. *Reading Teacher, 43,* 626–639.

Miller, D. (2002). *Reading with meaning.* Portland, ME: Stenhouse.

Mooney, M. (2004). *A book is a present: Selecting text for intentional teaching.* Katonah, NY: Richard C. Owens.

Nagy, W. (2003, October). *Complex causal links between vocabulary knowledge and reading comprehension: A rationale for a long-term, comprehensive approach to promoting vocabulary growth.* Paper presented at the Focus on Vocabulary Forum, Dallas, TX.

National Institute of Child Health and Human Development (NICHHD). (2001). *Report of the National Reading Panel: Teaching children to read. An evidence-based assessment of the scientific research literature on reading and its implications for reading instruction. Reports of the subgroups.* Washington, DC: National Institutes of Health.

Ogle, D. (1986). K-W-L: A teaching model that develops active reading of expository text. *Reading Teacher, 39,* 564–570.

Ohanian, S. (2002). *The great word catalogue.* Portsmouth, NH: Heinemann.

Pinnell, G. S., & Fountas, I. C. (1998). *Word matters: Teaching phonics and spelling in the reading/writing classroom.* Portsmouth, NH: Heinemann.

Routman, R. (1991). *Invitations.* Portsmouth, NH: Heinemann.

Routman, R. (2000). *Conversations.* Portsmouth, NH: Heinemann.

Routman, R. (2002). *Reading essentials.* Portsmouth, NH: Heinemann.

Wilde, S. (2000). *Miscue analysis made easy.* Portsmouth, NH: Heinemann.

Children's Books

Anonymous. (2003). The secret. In G. S. Pinnell & I. C. Fountas (Eds.), *Sing a song of poetry* (p. 230). Portsmouth, NH: Heinemann.

Cameron, A. (1989). *The stories Julian tells.* New York: Yearling.

Cherry, L. (1990). *The great kapok tree.* San Diego: Harcourt, Brace, Jovanovich.

Gibbons, G. (1994). *Nature's green umbrella: Tropical rain forests*. New York: Morrow Junior Books.

Hennessy, B. G. (1990). *The cake that Jake baked*. New York: Scholastic.

Landau, E. (1996). *Grassland mammals*. Danbury, CT: Children's Press.

Lobel, A. (1970). *Frog and toad are friends*. New York: HarperCollins.

Osborne, M. P. (1993). *Magic tree house: The knight at dawn*. New York: Random House.

Patrick, D. L. (1993). *Red dancing shoes*. New York: Harper Trophy.

Rylant, C. (1987). *Henry and Mudge: The first book*. New York: Simon & Schuster.

Rylant, C. (1994). *Mr. Putter and Tabby bake the cake*. San Diego: Harcourt Brace.

Steig, W. (1982). *Dr. DeSoto*. New York: Scholastic.

Tayntor, E. (1986). *Dive to the coral reefs*. New York: Crown.

Index

CORWIN
PRESS

The Corwin Press logo—a raven striding across an open book—represents the union of courage and learning. Corwin Press is committed to improving education for all learners by publishing books and other professional development resources for those serving the field of PreK–12 education. By providing practical, hands-on materials, Corwin Press continues to carry out the promise of its motto: **"Helping Educators Do Their Work Better."**